The Energy Squeeze

Canadian Policies for Survival

The Canadian Institute for Economic Policy has been established to engage in public discussion of fiscal, industrial and other related public policies designed to strengthen Canada in a rapidly changing international environment.

The Institute fulfills this mandate by sponsoring and undertaking studies pertaining to the economy of Canada and disseminating such studies. Its intention is to contribute in an innovative way to the development of public policy in Canada.

Other titles available in the Canadian Institute for Economic Policy Series are:

The Monetarist Counter-Revolution: A Critique of Canadian Monetary Policy 1975-1979
Arthur W. Donner and Douglas D. Peters

Canada's Crippled Dollar: An Analysis of International Trade and Our Troubled Balance of Payments
H. Lukin Robinson

Unemployment and Inflation: The Canadian Experience
Clarence L. Barber and John C. P. McCallum

How Ottawa Decides: Planning and Industrial Policy-Making 1968-1980
Richard D. French

Energy and Industry: The Potential of Energy Development Projects for Canadian Industry in the Eighties
Barry Beale

Canadian Institute for Economic Policy
Suite 409 350 Sparks St., Ottawa K1R 7S8

The Energy Squeeze

Canadian Policies for Survival

Bruce F. Willson

James Lorimer & Company, Publishers
in association with the
Canadian Institute for Economic Policy
Toronto 1980

The opinions expressed in this study are those of the author alone and are not intended to represent those of any organization with which he may be associated.

Copyright © 1980 by Canadian Institute For Economic Policy

ISBN 0-88862-302-X paper
ISBN 0-88862-303-8 cloth
6 5 4 3 2 1   80 81 82 83 84 85 86

Canadian Cataloguing in Publication Data
Willson, Bruce F., 1921–
    The energy squeeze

ISBN 0-88862-302-X pa.   ISBN 0-88862-303-8 bd.

1. Energy policy – Canada.   I. Title.

HD9502.C32W54   333.79′0971   C80-094115-2

Additional copies of this book
may be purchased from:

James Lorimer & Company, Publishers
Egerton Ryerson Memorial Building
35 Britain Street,
Toronto M5A 1R7, Ontario

Printed and bound in Canada

Contents

Tables and Charts

Foreword

Bruce Willson's study is a panoramic view of our energy crisis. It surveys not only our oil and gas prospects to the year 2025, but the situation we face in respect to coal, hydro-electricity, nuclear energy and solar energy. Only a synthesis of this scope, based on the best official data available, can set the stage for what is still to come – a comprehensive and long-term national energy policy. Willson's is an extraordinary and courageous effort by a single individual in an area where governments and royal commissions have been reluctant to tread, except through short-term and piecemeal analyses.

The picture is unmistakably grim and foreboding. Even the most modest assumptions about the rate of growth of our economy will require that we consume substantially larger supplies of energy by the turn of the century if a technological society is to be sustained. Yet as the charts reveal, the cumulative supply of energy from conventional non-renewable sources falls away by that time as dramatically as a ski slope. Short of a wartime situation, it is difficult to conceive of a long-term energy policy being formulated under more stringent difficulties.

The discovery of substantial offshore deposits of oil may give us a reprieve over the medium term, but they do not alter the long-term prospects. Reliable data on new proven reserves along our east coast are still lacking and Willson's data already include some provision for new discoveries. Perhaps the present analysis may have to be modified by larger discoveries than were expected, but the challenge of a long-term energy policy remains, nevertheless, a very urgent item on our present agenda.

Willson is critical both of our previous policies and of the present focus of the energy debate. Problems of constitutional jurisdiction over resources, the "high-price scenario" versus the "low-price scenario", the role of the multinationals, are contentious issues on which Willson declares himself forthrightly. But he has not hesitated to grasp the nettle and offers us a comprehensive program that meets the situation.

Its central features are a cost-based approach to energy pricing and a new National Energy Corporation designed to mobilize a truly national effort around the exploitation of the tar sands. Willson recognizes that such a program is open to substantial modification and adaptation as rapidly changing circumstances may warrant.

It is a time to set aside the various dogmas and rules of thumb to which we may normally be inclined. Whether we are advocates of "world prices" or "made-in-Canada prices", of provincial or federal control of resources, of private sector versus public sector initiatives, our positions must meet a pragmatic test that flows from the present analysis: How are we to assure an adequate supply of energy for Canada beyond the turn of the century? What institutions are most likely to achieve this task?

The directors of the Canadian Institute for Economic Policy do not pretend to a unanimity of view on these far-reaching issues. While we are pleased to publish Bruce Willson's study as an eminent contribution to the public debate, the analysis and conclusions remain the responsibility of the author.

Abraham Rotstein
Vice-Chairman
Canadian Institute for Economic Policy

Preface

In recent decades, Canada and the industrialized world have been running on huge power subsidies derived from the production and utilization of fossil fuels stored in the earth's crust. These deposits were created by solar power playing on the surface of the earth for billions of years. The reserves are finite, depleting, and in Canada are largely controlled by entities whose objectives do not always coincide with the national public interest. As a result, Canadians will soon be facing severe energy shortages, as well as high rates of inflation induced by arbitrary and largely ineffective price increases. This study endeavours to set the emerging Canadian crisis in oil and gas supply and pricing in a national and worldwide context. In this way it is hoped the reader will be able to understand the true nature of the energy supply problems facing the country and to make sense of the day-to-day developments in relation to this vital aspect of the Canadian economy.

Historically, Canadian policy has been to rely on the private sector to provide the national economy and individual citizens with essential supplies of oil and gas at reasonable prices. That such a policy has failed is evidenced by declining supplies and skyrocketing prices. Domestic entrepreneurs are taking advantage of growing worldwide shortages and the existence of an international cartel to export more of Canada's limited reserves and to insist on much higher prices for Canadian production. Government policy to date has been to accede to them, apparently in the hope that something favourable will happen that will lead to a solution.

There is every indication, however, that the Canadian oil and gas supply outlook will continue to deteriorate. If so, society could well be immobilized. Furthermore, a policy of even faster price increases will only aggravate the already unwarranted prices Canadians are being forced to pay for their own resources. As this study demonstrates, the massive price increases to date have been unable to stem the trend towards awesome energy supply deficits. Additionally, the quintupling of the domestic wellhead price for oil and the 900 per cent increase in that for natural gas have fuelled inflation since 1973. Recent federal government forecasts of a still higher inflation rate reflect the impact of potentially even steeper price hikes resulting from heavy pressure from the oil industry and the Alberta government.

This study focuses primarily on the oil and gas sectors because these two energy sources provide nearly two-thirds of the country's primary energy supply. The prospective supply/demand balances for uranium, coal, and hydroelectric power are also examined. Sections on conservation and renewable energy indicate some of the potential that would exist if they were to receive adequate attention from government and industry.

The main conclusion of this study is that sweeping new energy policies, based on sound planning and equitable principles along with a basic understanding of the nature of the energy problems confronting the nation, are essential. The study suggests new policies and outlines a fresh approach to national energy supply planning to help overcome the approaching energy squeeze.

Acknowledgements

This book, which embodies the knowledge, experience, and understanding generated during my thirty-five years in Canadian energy industries, also reflects the encouragement and assistance of many individuals and friends and I am indebted to them. I undertook the study at the request of the Canadian Institute for Economic Policy, whose chairman is the Honourable Walter L. Gordon. Members of the Institute's executive committee – particularly Mr. Gordon, Professor Abraham Rotstein, and Senator Maurice Lamontagne – have been especially helpful with their specific suggestions and their understanding of the lengthy time required for the preparation of the manuscript. Their ongoing concern for the future of Canada was a constant inspiration for me – an engineer, not a writer or academic by profession – to complete this work.

Economist Terrence Burrell, initially with Middleton Associates and later with his own research and consulting firm Victor and Burrell, was of great assistance in the preparation of the sections on energy demand, coal, and renewable energy forms. His constructive criticism of the entire document resulted in improvements in both the organization of the material and its final presentation.

I am particularly grateful to Professor Ian McDougall of Osgoode Hall Law School for his advice on the issues surrounding the legal aspects of federal and provincial jurisdiction over resource development. His comments as a reviewer of the entire text, along with those of Professor Norbert Berkowitz of the Department of Mineral Engineering of the University of Alberta, Dr. John Helliwell of the Department of Economics, University of British Columbia, John Shepherd, director of the Institute and Professor Andrew Thompson, director of the Westwater Research Centre at the University of British Columbia were most valuable. Understandably, not every reviewer supported all of the specific policies advocated, but their comments and criticisms enabled me to test my theories and proposed solutions.

Diane Nelles as editor brought coherence and readability to my engineering-style report writing and I am most grateful to her for her important contribution to the study. Diana Murray co-ordinated the typing of the several drafts. Her unfailing co-operation was of particular help.

Last, but by no means least, my wife Joan remained always cheerful during the many months of my being underfoot while I worked from our home on the research, writing, and revisions and wrestled with the rather complex and multifaceted issues that energy policy generates today. The completion of this project is as much a credit to her sympathetic and understanding ways as it is to any other single factor.

Introduction

1

Our planet has existed for about four billion years. While the exact nature of its creation may be somewhat in doubt, we know that it has evolved with time until today it is populated by many kinds of ecological systems. Each of them has modified and conditioned itself to a wide variety of environmental situations. All this time the sun has been pouring energy on the surface of the earth to create the marine life and forests that have been transformed as the result of high temperatures and pressures into the petroleum and coal deposits known today.

Mankind appeared about one and a half million years ago. Only during the past ten thousand years, however, has he learned to manipulate his environment. Early in the period agriculture became possible as man first harnessed and concentrated solar energy. He used wind to power sailboats and to propel windmills, and he used falling water to drive his grist mills. Only relatively recently, as industrialization proceeded, did man begin to develop entirely new sources of energy and bases for power, exploiting coal, oil, and other stored energy sources. Until now supplies have been of such magnitude that excess energy has been available for further exploration and development of still more fossil fuels and, up to recently, the trend has been for energy reserves to rise in parallel with consumption.

Material progress has occurred during a mere moment in time compared with the long evolutionary period of the previous hundreds of millions of years. Today the great quantities of fossil fuels required to power our societies will exhaust available non-renewable energy forms in decades or a very few centuries at best – an infinitesimal interval during which to dissipate a priceless heritage. Industrialized society's relentless drive for physical growth, still higher living standards, and ever-increasing profits is taking place at the expense of generations to come.

At the same time, man is creating a huge new ecological system with inputs and outputs that never before existed. New products such as

1

insecticides, detergents, and a variety of industrial, organic, and nuclear wastes are affecting natural systems in ways that cannot be predicted totally but are clearly adverse to nature's long-term stability. Man is also disrupting land surfaces as he floods new areas for hydro projects and heads onto the northern permafrost in search of oil. All of these activities have unsettling effects on the long-established systems of nature, creating new imbalances to which nature has had virtually no time to adjust. While there is growing awareness of the inherent dangers to the environment, the problems created are a long way from solution.

Man's shift from his long-time role as a relatively minor component of natural systems – as a hunter and gatherer – to his present position as the predominant factor of modern industrial society is a direct result of the rapid increase of his energy supply and power support. It is within this context that the questions of energy and environmental policies must be faced. Material progress has become so rapid and dramatic in the twentieth century that many people believe virtually anything is possible. What is not well understood is that all these changes have followed as a direct result of increases in energy supply.

Only recently has there been a growing awareness of this dependency and recognition of the finite and diminishing extent of the non-renewable energy resources that have been vitalizing modern society. It is now generally accepted that for all practical purposes worldwide supplies of petroleum will run out within the lifetime of those born today. This has finally led to genuine concern on the part of governments of both producing and consuming nations. For those countries without domestic supplies, oil and its byproducts have become increasingly scarce and expensive. Petroleum is not only the principal form of energy in use today, but it is also the primary base from which so many valuable synthetic polymers for plastics and pharmaceuticals are derived. Therefore, it is crucial that reserves throughout the world be managed with the utmost care and concern for the future. Though it is hardly necessary to enumerate the myriad uses of energy in an industrialized economy or to detail the degree to which individuals have become dependent on adequate and reliable supplies of energy at reasonable prices, an examination of Canada's energy consumption and supply patterns is instructive and indicates the enormity of the problems confronting this country.

Canada's Energy Consumption and Supply Patterns

Energy consumption in Canada rose from about 200 trillion Btus in 1870 to 9 quadrillion Btus in 1978, a more than fortyfold increase that

2

corresponds to an annual growth rate of 3.5 per cent.[1] Underlying the huge increase were two major shifts in supply.

At the time of Confederation, Canadians derived over 90 per cent of their inanimate energy supplies from wood. By 1900 coal and coke had become the most important source of energy, directly supplying more than half of the energy consumed in Canada. This share continued to rise into the 1920s when coal and coke clearly dominated all other forms of energy supply, and the contribution of wood fell below 20 per cent of total consumption. By then petroleum and related products accounted for nearly 10 per cent of energy consumed, already double that supplied by electricity and natural gas.[2]

As recently as 1950 coal and coke still provided close to half of the energy used in Canada. However, by this time the share of both petroleum and electricity had overtaken that of wood, with petroleum and natural gas capturing slightly over 30 per cent of the total market. Within a short period, their share surpassed that of coal and coke and by 1960 they supplied over half of the energy used in Canada. Petroleum's share of the energy market now appears to have peaked at about 45 per cent, while that of natural gas probably has plateaued around 20 per cent. Electricity, whose share has grown steadily since the turn of the century, contributes about 25 per cent or so of Canada's energy supplies (Table 1-1).

TABLE 1-1
PRIMARY ENERGY CONSUMPTION, BY SOURCE, CANADA, 1950–77

	1950	1960	1970	1975	1977
	(Per cent)				
Petroleum	29.8	48.6	48.1	46.8	44.7
Natural gas	2.5	9.0	16.5	18.8	18.8
Coal and coke	47.6	14.7	10.7	8.0	8.9
Hydro-electricity	20.1	27.7	24.6	24.9	24.6
Nuclear electricity	–	–	.1	1.5	3.0
	$(10^{12}$ Btus)				
Total	2,493	3,671	6,328	7,826	8,267

Source: J.E. Gander and F.W. Belaire, *Energy Futures for Canadians* (LEAP) (Ottawa: Energy, Mines and Resources Canada 1978), p. 303.

Thus in the space of one hundred years Canada has gone from a reliance on essentially renewable sources of energy (wood) to dependence on non-renewable fossil fuels – first coal and then oil and gas –

3

supplemented to a degree by hydro and nuclear electricity. At present nuclear electricity contributes around 3 per cent of the energy consumed in Canada, but its share is increasing. In view of the growing awareness and concern about, as well as the finite nature of, Canadian and world supplies of depleting non-renewable resources, it is entirely possible that in another hundred years the energy economy will return to almost total reliance on renewable forms of energy.

The most recent trends are very important. In Table 1-2, which shows the total secondary energy[3] consumed and the share of each major sector, three significant trends stand out: overall demand doubled in only fifteen years; the rate of growth in secondary energy demand fell from an average annual rate of 5.5 per cent between 1960 and 1970 to 3.4 per cent between 1970 and 1975; and the share of energy consumed in the commercial sector increased. This reflects the energy-intensive nature of economic growth, the economic slowdown in the seventies compared with sixties, and the continuing urbanization of Canadian society. Future energy shortages and high prices will have profound effects on these trends.

TABLE 1-2
SECONDARY ENERGY CONSUMPTION, BY SECTOR, CANADA
1960–75

	Share of energy consumed		
	1960	1970	1975
	(Per cent)		
Energy supply industries	7.3	8.6	8.7
Transportation	25.5	24.3	26.2
Domestic and farm	24.4	20.8	19.8
Commercial	8.5	14.1	12.3
Industrial	34.3	32.2	33.0
	(10^{12} Btus)		
Total	2,920	4,971	5,878

Source: Statistics Canada, *Detailed Energy Supply and Demand in Canada*, Cat: 57-207.

Until the Middle East oil embargo and the quadrupling of oil prices by the Organization of Petroleum Exporting Countries (OPEC) in 1973, Canadians had been led to believe that their country possessed almost boundless energy supplies. In 1971 they had been told by their Minister of Energy, Mines and Resources that "Canada's total oil reserves were 469 billion barrels at the end of 1970, while total natural gas reserves were 726 trillion cubic feet. At 1970 rates of production, these reserves represent 923 years' supply for oil and 392 years' for gas." When queried about the accuracy of his statements, the Minister quoted as his sources of information the National Energy Board and the Canadian Petroleum Association, an industry association dominated by the major multinational oil companies.[4]

Two years later, in March 1973, the Annual Report of Imperial Oil Limited for the previous year provided further assurances: "In the current debate, the export of Canada's energy resources is being questioned; in effect, we are being urged to bank our petroleum resources. Canada is not in any way deficient in energy resources. Our present energy reserves, using present technology, are sufficient for our requirements for several hundred years."[5]

On the strength of these statements and other similar positions taken by government and industry spokesmen, it is not surprising that the Canadian public was led to the conclusion that energy supply was the least of the country's worries. Large-scale oil and gas exports by the petroleum industry were undertaken because U.S. markets continued to grow and American companies, whose domestic supplies had peaked, looked northward and contracted for Canadian production.

Individuals who expressed concern about the true magnitude of Canada's established oil and gas reserves and their limited capability for meeting future domestic energy requirements, let alone large export markets, were looked upon as shortsighted pessimists, lacking in vision. When confronted with the irrefutable decline in petroleum life indices, the oil industry pointed to the vast frontier areas and claimed huge potential oil and gas production from yet untapped regions. This remains the industry's position, despite more than ten years of largely unsuccessful frontier exploration effort undertaken primarily at the expense of the Canadian taxpayer.

Generally governments, with their interests in royalty and taxation revenues, have supported the industry position. While the National Energy Board, after some strenuous public intervention, vetoed additional gas export permits in 1971 on the grounds that the reserves proposed for export were clearly needed in Canada, the rate of flow of oil exports to the United States was not reduced until 1974. Meanwhile, gas exports continued at the level approved in 1970, amounting to about 40 per cent of marketed production throughout the 1970s.

Following the 1973 OPEC actions, the Canadian oil industry mounted a totally different platform. Canadian representatives of the oil companies at that time acknowledged what their critics had long contended – namely, that Canada's proved and available oil and gas reserves were indeed quite limited. However, once again, they implied that there was no need to worry about adequacy of future supply.

5

Imperial Oil in its 1973 Annual Report released in March 1974 stated that "within the next 10 years, production rates from existing reserves in Western Canada will be inadequate to supply markets now being served, and new sources of supply must be ready to start delivering energy when this decline begins. The sources are available."[6]

But the emphasis by the companies shifted to the need for higher prices. Even though after-tax profits had leaped over 40 per cent from 1972 to the pivotal year of 1973 for both the Imperial and Shell oil companies, they expressed concern about government "takes" in the form of royalties and taxes. The argument advanced by company spokesmen then was that oil and gas supplies were "price elastic," and that all that was needed to make Canada self-sufficient in energy was to increase the price and industry "cash flow" and the supplies would be forthcoming.

Government energy planners accepted the industry's arguments. The federal government's study, *An Energy Policy for Canada*, forecast that conventional oil reserves would increase by 800 per cent (from 10 billion barrels to 90 billion barrels) if the price were increased to $8 a barrel at the east coast of North America.[7] It further projected that, at $8 a barrel, another 60 billion barrels from mineable tar sands deposits would be economically producible, giving Canada total recoverable reserves of 150 billion barrels at that price. This was more than fifteen times the level of proved oil reserves at the time.

However, conventional crude oil reserves began to decline in 1969, when proved crude reserves peaked at 8.6 billion barrels.[8] Faced with falling conventional reserves, reductions in domestic oil production, a need for conservation through lowered consumption, extreme pressure from the producing provinces, and skilled lobbying by the oil industry, the federal government opted for a "high-price scenario" as one of its energy policy planks.[9] Under this policy the domestic wellhead price for crude oil escalated from about $3.00 per barrel at the beginning of 1973 to $14.75 as of January 1, 1980. At the same time the wellhead price of natural gas skyrocketed from about 17 cents per thousand cubic feet in early 1973 to an average of approximately $1.65 in the latter part of 1979 (see Charts 3-6 and 3-11).

While these unprecedented price increases were taking place, proved oil reserves continued their decline. By the end of 1979, despite improved recovery techniques and a few discoveries, proved reserves were down for the tenth year in a row to 5.7 billion barrels, a decline of 35 per cent from 1969.[10] Proved and geographically available gas reserves at the beginning of 1979 were about 10 per cent higher than those in the previous peak year of 1971.[11] Overall, however, the supply situation does not remotely resemble that promised by the petroleum industry or

6

the picture painted in the federal government studies that forecast abundant reserves in return for public acceptance of high energy prices.

To date Canada has relied almost totally on the private sector to develop the country's energy resources. But there is a special problem involved in this reliance because the principal oil and gas producing companies operating in Canada are foreign controlled. The exception today is the federal government's own oil company, Petro-Canada, which commenced operations in 1976 and is probably now Canada's ninth largest producer. One reason the energy supply outlook for Canada is particularly critical is largely a result of the export and other policies pursued by the petroleum industry. Foreign controlled companies have their own commercial and financial objectives, and they operate under policies initiated and approved by their parent companies. Recognition of this reality is fundamental to the design of Canadian energy policy. The analysis of future energy requirements in this study demonstrates the need for Canada to manage and control its own energy affairs.

Canada and the Energy Problem

At long last there appears to be a growing awareness among politicians that this country faces critical energy shortages. World events, lineups for gasoline in the United States, and threatened heating oil shortages in Canada have combined to awaken political leaders to the gloomy outlook for the 1980s. While previous federal governments appeared to accept the impression left by the oil industry and the province of Alberta that somehow the ominous situation could be resolved by massive price increases for domestic crude oil and natural gas, the government now appears to recognize that energy policy is complex and is beginning to devote the attention warranted to energy issues.

The principal submission of this study is that what will probably prove to be the most formidable obstacle to the maintenance of a prospering economy and reasonable living standards for Canadians is the future availability of adequate supplies of all forms of energy at reasonable prices. The prime purpose of this study is to quantify the magnitude of the challenge facing the nation in trying to meet future energy needs and to suggest a method whereby the twin goals of energy self-sufficiency and a sustainable energy future may be attained through a national approach to energy supply planning and demand management. When approaching the question of how best to design a national plan to ensure a healthy future for this country a logical place to start is to take inventory of our own reserves and resources and to evaluate this country's strengths and weaknesses.

Canada is fortunate in that it possesses a per capita endowment of natural resources that is probably second to none in the world. By world standards deposits of tar sands and heavy oils are massive. The nation's coal reserves are also highly significant. These resources will be required on an unprecedented scale if future energy needs are to be met. Their availability and use will assist materially in tiding Canada over until technology enables us to develop suitable alternate forms of renewable energy, until the present energy-intensive industrialized economy can be wound down to a supportable level, or until these elements combine to curb our requirements for fossil fuels. Canada's further advantages include a democratic political system that is generally responsive to the national interest; a modern educational system that is able to serve the requirements of the professions and labour; a market economy that offers the entrepreneur rewards for his risk-taking and ingenuity; and a stable currency that allows this country to participate actively in world trade.

While these assets are tremendously important, we are also faced with some serious problems. Among them is the fact that Canada is a large and cold northern country whose population is small and dispersed. This means that we require long, high-cost transportation systems to reach the relatively small domestic market and large supplies of fuels merely to keep us warm. Both of these factors mean that Canada is comparatively energy inefficient. The geographically uneven distribution of energy resources and market requirements also leads to relatively high transportation costs for delivery of energy supplies, particularly to and from the more remote sections of the country.

We also have an economy and a way of life that is dependent on hydrocarbon fuels for 65 per cent of our energy needs. At the same time, the country is faced with rapidly declining life indices for both petroleum and natural gas (see Charts 3-6 and 3-11). Already Canada has a large deficit in crude oil supplies and is required to import 30 per cent of its requirements from offshore suppliers of varying degrees of reliability. Similar deficiencies for natural gas are virtually inevitable in the foreseeable future, given current export policies and the low rate of additions to proved reserves.

Historically we have been dependent on the private sector for the procurement and delivery of sufficient supplies of hydrocarbon energy to meet the needs of the Canadian economy. In the final analysis, however, the private energy companies are primarily interested in maximizing profits rather than in ensuring that Canada's energy needs are met under all circumstances. In the past, when supplies were adequate and competitive factors existed, the approach worked in reasonably equitable fashion. It does not work well when supplies are tight or

8

inadequate and positions of domination and monopoly control are exploited by entrenched interests. This is the situation today in Canada's energy industries.

The problem is exacerbated by the fact that the industry is dominated by subsidiaries of multinational companies whose duties and loyalties lie with their parent company rather than with Canada's national interest. Among other things this means a branch-plant orientation of the industry resulting in limited research and development, technical innovation, and management skills. It also means that increasingly large amounts of dividends, interest, management fees, and royalties flow out of the country to service the growing level of foreign ownership. Foreign ownership and control of the industry are partially responsible for the fact that the United States, with its huge energy appetite and its rapidly dwindling and largely depleted indigenous oil and gas reserves, has been able to influence energy developments in Canada for its own advantage.

The federal system of government in this country is a major disadvantage in dealing with overall problems of energy supply. Ownership of natural resources rests with the provinces, and this has tended to complicate the co-ordinated planning and development of resource related projects necessary for the country as a whole. More recently it has also contributed to regional tensions. In the face of this system it is difficult to understand why some politicians believe it is logical to rely on provincial control of resources and a market economy to solve the country's energy problems in the most efficient and equitable manner. Partly for this reason too, governments and bureaucracies have failed to understand the seriousness of the problems facing the country, have lacked the will to tackle them, or both.

That Canadians have been conditioned to believe this country possesses huge stores of accessible oil and gas reserves is another problem that adds to Canada's energy dilemma. In the past, industry analysis and government policy have been based on a short- to medium-term outlook that seldom extends beyond the 1990s. This tends to mask the real seriousness of Canada's position. In order to grasp the energy problems Canadians face, it is necessary to look beyond the short and medium ranges and examine the developing situation at least through the first quarter of the next century.

Recognition of these problems serves to stress the magnitude of the task confronting Canada in designing and implementing industrial and energy strategies that will stabilize a deteriorating situation in the face of difficult odds. This study examines today's supply position in terms of this perspective. It outlines the adequacy over the medium and long terms of Canada's energy reserves and economically recoverable resources as they are presently understood and discusses trends in discovery rates and projections of market requirements. It concludes by outlining specific recommendations for energy policy and planning. The study urges the development and implementation of positive energy policies that would reverse the present deteriorating situation and which, if implemented, would help ensure that our essential energy needs for the next thirty years would be met in the most efficient and equitable manner. While there are too many uncertainties and unknowns for definitive planning beyond such an interval, the direction is clear. Present-day practices and high levels of energy use are unsustainable. A start must be made immediately to develop a stable energy economy.

Throughout the preparation of this study I have been acutely conscious of the difficulties involved in presenting a comprehensive profile of Canada's energy dilemma during what inevitably is a fluid and evolving situation. The risks of any such analysis becoming out-of-date are high even though industry discovery trends are examined over sizable time periods and compared with finding experience in other jurisdictions. Unfortunately, whether commercial oil or gas reserves exist at Hibernia, Ben Nevis, the Beaufort Sea or the high Eastern Arctic is still uncertain. The determination of this must await the drilling of many more frontier wells and the completion of complex engineering and economic feasibility studies. The short drilling seasons and the slow pace of the exploratory effort combine to frustrate the gathering of adequate data for reliable reserve estimates. Results in 1979 were encouraging in that two oil and two natural gas discoveries were reported out of the twenty-eight frontier exploratory wells drilled. Unfortunately, twenty wells were dry and abandoned while four others were suspended to be re-entered in 1980.[12]

In addition to the frontier potential, strong possibilities exist for energy production from the deeper tar sands deposits utilizing in situ techniques not yet developed, and from the liquefaction or gasification of coal using present or future technology. The question for today's energy planner is what weight to assign to possible new sources of energy supply where so many unknowns and uncertainties exist.

A study such as this one must begin by dealing with energy reserves as they are known at the present time and this has been done using primarily National Energy Board (NEB) and Alberta Energy Resources Conservation Board (AERCB) data. However, the reader's attention should be drawn to the fact that anticipated new discoveries in the western Canada sedimentary basin are already included in the estimates of future oil and gas producibility that have been adopted. For example, Charts 3-7, 3-14, and 3-17 all show the hoped for production from future additions to conventional reserves.

Discoveries of oil or gas in excess of these amounts will, of course, extend the date at which critical shortages will begin to occur, provided equivalent volumes are not exported in the meantime. Based on Canada's past record, this is an important proviso. But recent frontier discoveries do not, in my view, alter the basic policy measures that will be needed over the longer term to deal directly and forcefully with our looming difficulties. Moreover, the opposite danger should not be ignored – namely, that a mood of complacency or even euphoria will accompany these single well finds, and that such a mood will tempt the country and its leaders to turn away from the stringent decisions needed in the near future if an effective national energy policy is to be brought into being.

Energy Demand 2

Any comprehensive study of energy policy must compare projections of future energy demand with estimates of anticipated economically available sources of supply. Only after such comparisons have been made can problem areas be identified and quantified and policies designed to circumvent or overcome them. This chapter examines energy demand; the next two chapters analyse energy supply. Obviously the shape of our energy policies will depend very much on how much energy we will want or need to consume in the future. The greater Canada's future energy requirements, the greater the demands that will be placed on our energy supply infrastructure. By 1978 Canadians consumed a total of about 9 quadrillion Btus (quads) of primary energy.[1] The question is how much energy are we likely to need in the future?

In the past, Canadian energy consumption has increased at a significant pace. Primary energy consumption has risen at an average annual rate of about 3.5 per cent since Confederation. This growth accelerated after the Second World War and especially after 1960, so that between 1960 and 1970, for example, primary energy use bounded ahead at 5.6 per cent per year. Between 1970 and 1977 demand growth slowed somewhat to 3.9 per cent because of the combined and interrelated effects of the energy price rises and the economic downturn that began in 1973.

But is the past a good guide to future energy requirements? If so, which past period is the future most likely to reflect? As stated in Chapter 1, it is necessary to look at least as far into the future as the first quarter of the next century in order to understand better the energy problems Canadians face. Any attempt to predict is fraught with uncertainty and the further into the future the prediction is extended, the greater the uncertainty becomes. Many of the basic determinants of energy demand can significantly change of their own accord over the next forty-five years. Another important consideration, which fundamentally adds to the uncertainty, is that energy demand levels can be altered to a certain degree by the choices that are made, not just by separately motivated individuals but also through the political process and through government action, such as conservation programs and supply allocations.

While a good deal of work has been done on energy projections by different public and private bodies, such as the federal Department of Energy, Mines and Resources, the National Energy Board, and individual oil companies, until fairly recently these forecasts have tended to focus on the short to medium term. Thus there is still much room for longer term analyses, such as in this study, and for a clear evaluation of the anticipated effects of all the factors that might alter the supply/demand equation. Before proceeding with that task, it is useful to examine some of the forecasts that are available.

Short-Range Forecasts

One of the early studies of the Canadian energy situation, published by the federal Department of Energy, Mines and Resources in 1976, was *An Energy Strategy for Canada.*[2] That document put forward two scenarios for the growth in energy demand for the period to 1990. The "high growth" scenario assumed a 4.3 per cent annual growth rate; the "low growth" scenario, 3.7 per cent.

Later the National Energy Board (NEB) in its 1978 *Oil Report,* forecast an annual growth rate in primary energy demand of about 2.9 per cent to 1995.[3] In its 1979 *Gas Report* the NEB upped the projection to 3.1 per cent growth each year to the end of the century, which would put Canada's energy consumption at 17 quads in the year 2000.[4] Both these projections were based on an aggregate approach that involves three basic steps: identification of the key determinants of energy demand, such as population, per capita income, and energy prices; evaluation, using statistical techniques, of how these determinants have affected demand in the past; and projections of how the key determinants are likely to behave in the future considering available information about past patterns. This approach has much to recommend it. However, the statistics directly link the energy projections to how energy demand has reacted to past changes in income levels, energy prices, and available supply. If these historical responses are not a good guide to how energy demand can or will respond in the future, then the overall demand projections will be misleading.

Given the major changes that have occurred since 1973 in the price and perceived availability of all conventional energy sources and petroleum in particular, the period prior to the mid-1970s is not likely to serve as an adequate indicator of future demand. The past is likely to prove an even less reliable guide once we begin to explore the question of how much energy demand could be reduced while maintaining an acceptable standard of living.

The amount and type of energy consumed at any time is determined by a wide range of factors including, of course, the quantity and cost of different forms of energy that are available. In the simplest terms, energy demand depends upon population size and per capita energy use. Per capita energy consumption in turn is directly derived from the quantity of products and services consumed that themselves require energy and from the efficiency with which energy is used in providing these services and producing these products. This is an important point; what we have come to characterize as our standard of living and lifestyle is not totally determined by our direct consumption of energy. They are dependent upon our consumption of goods and services of all types. The overall efficiency with which energy is used in the production and consumption of these goods and services is a crucial mediating link, therefore, between energy consumption and our standard of living.

Overall efficiency here means not just the efficiency with which energy is converted for final use in a specific process – for example, the efficiency with which an oil burner converts fuel oil to heat – it includes as well the total design of processes and equipment, buildings, and cities. A good example of the concept is provided by the recently completed Ontario Hydro office building in Toronto, which was designed to provide a range of facilities and services typical of a commercial structure while minimizing energy use. It consumes about 65 million Btus per square foot annually, while the average for office buildings is three to four times that figure.

A newer approach to projecting energy demand puts existing and potential energy efficiency at the centre of its analysis. This approach examines in detail energy end-use demands in each sector with a view to identifying potential energy conserving changes that would not affect the services delivered and would also be economic. To be undertaken comprehensively for the economy as a whole, this approach requires a great deal of highly disaggregated work.

The Department of Energy, Mines and Resources, in its document titled *Energy Conservation in Canada* released in 1977, presented the results of such an analysis, though it only examined a limited number of conservation possibilities. It took as its starting point the changes in population and energy price forecasts underlying the *Energy Strategy* projection for the low-growth energy demand scenario. *Energy Conservation* concluded that significant decreases in levels of energy consumption could be achieved in each of the residential, commercial, indus-

14

trial, and transportation sectors of the economy by 1990. The report suggested that annual energy growth could be cut from the earlier figure of 3.7 per cent to 2 per cent over the period to 1990; this is equivalent to a 20 per cent decrease in the primary energy requirements projected for 1990.[5]

Savings would vary from sector to sector. For example, in the residential sector the study estimated a 21 per cent reduction in 1990 end-use energy consumption to be possible through upgrading of insulation in existing buildings, raising of insulation standards for new buildings, lowering of thermostats to 21°C in the daytime and 18°C at night, and improving burner efficiency. Similar measures in the commercial sector would yield a 28 per cent decrease in that sector's 1990 end-use energy consumption. In the transportation sector, measures such as the adoption of U.S. fuel economy standards for automobiles and moderately increased use of public transit in urban areas would bring about a decline in end-use energy consumption of 28 per cent. The report assumed that, in the industrial sector, no special measures would be taken beyond those likely to result from the price increases assumed in the *Energy Strategy* 3.7 per cent energy consumption growth scenario. Consequently, industry is assumed to cut back about 2 per cent from the level assumed in *An Energy Strategy*. The energy supply industries, whose energy consumption levels depend basically upon the amount of energy consumed in the other sectors, were expected to lower their energy consumption by 29 per cent.

The report acknowledged that an even greater degree of energy conservation was possible by 1990, since a number of feasible conservation measures were not considered in the analysis. The report lists a number of these, including improved energy efficiency in household and commercial appliances, more efficient lighting and the reduction of unnecessary lighting levels, greater vehicle pooling, improvements in road and air freight load factors, expanded use of diesel engines for automobiles, increased recycling of materials in industrial production, expansion in the industrial cogeneration of heat and electricity, improvements in the agricultural and food systems, and greater implementation of district heating systems utilizing waste heat and heat from burning of urban waste. In addition, the *Energy Conservation* report acknowledged that the further beyond 1990 the analysis is taken, the greater the potential for energy demand reductions:

> The options for energy conservation after 1990 are far wider than for the period from now to 1990. There is the opportunity not only to alter major portions of the capital structure – the replacement, say of a large share of short-haul air traffic by rapid rail systems – but to plan in such a way that the whole structure of energy demands is different.[6]

15

Longer Range Forecasts

One of the few longer range energy projections for Canada was published in a 1978 report entitled *Energy Futures for Canadians,* which has come to be known as the LEAP report. Others include a study by Amory Lovins and one prepared as a background paper for the LEAP report. We consider them here briefly.

The LEAP report drew from a wide range of sources including aggregated projections derived from econometric analyses and the possibilities for energy conservation included in the *Energy Conservation* report. After an examination of a number of different possibilities, the authors of the LEAP report suggested that Canada's primary energy demand would be 16 quads by 2000 and 20 quads in 2025, which is equivalent to an annual growth rate of 2.8 per cent between 1975 and 2000 and 0.9 per cent from 2000 to 2025.

The demographic and economic assumptions underlying the LEAP forecasts, as well as the projections of primary and secondary energy demand growth, are presented in Table 2-1. From the table it is clear that the projected population growth rate of 0.7 per cent annually is less than half the 1960–75 rate of 1.6 per cent and would lead to a population of 33 million Canadians by 2025. As a result of a lower population increase, the aging of the populace, and the maturing of the economy, LEAP suggests that future GNP growth rates can be expected to fall to about half the rate of the recent past. Similarly, the rate of increase in real income is expected to be about one-half that of the past. While some concern might be expressed with such reductions, the authors consider them to be generally satisfactory, given their assumptions of a more mature society and the difficult economic times ahead.

As a target to be achieved through planning and energy conservation, LEAP projects a 50 per cent reduction in the growth rate in the demand for both primary and secondary energy in the period to 2000 followed by a further two-thirds cut in the 2000–25 period. Nevertheless, primary energy requirements would grow from 8 quads in 1975 to 16 quads in 2000 and to 20 quads in 2025; secondary energy demand would increase from 5.5 to 12.5 quads over the whole period. The lower rate of increase in primary energy demand than in GNP indicates an increase in efficiency in energy use and the anticipated impact of conservation. Major reductions in the ratio of primary energy demand to GNP are forecast. The authors advocate much higher energy prices to ensure more careful use of secondary energy, though they do not directly relate the impact of such a policy on economic growth and living standards. To date, however, there is little indication that high

16

TABLE 2-1
ECONOMIC AND ENERGY DEMAND FORECASTS, CANADA, 1960–2025

	1975	2000	2025	Annual rate of change (Per cent)			
				1960-1975	1975-2000	2000-2025	1975-2025
Population (millions)	22.8	30.0	33.0	1.6	1.2	0.5	0.7
GNP (billions $ 1975)	161	375	560	5.0	3.4	1.6	2.5
Personal disposable income (billions $ 1975)	108	250	375	5.3	3.4	1.7	2.6
GNP per capita ($ 1975)	7,061	12,500	16,970	3.2	2.3	1.1	1.7
Primary energy (quads)	8.0	16.0	20.0	5.3	2.8	0.9	1.9
Secondary energy (quads)	5.5	10.0	12.5	5.3	2.4	0.9	1.7
Primary energy/GNP (1975 = 100)	100	86	72	0.4	-0.6	-0.7	-0.7

Source: J. E. Gander and F.W. Belaire, *Energy Futures for Canadians* (LEAP) (Ottawa: Energy, Mines and Resources Canada, 1978) p. 73.

prices have much effect in reducing consumption in industrialized nations.

The forecasts of energy demand in the LEAP report are lower than the historical rates and lower as well than many of the other projections published before the LEAP report was released in early 1979.[7] The LEAP figures are not, however, the lowest projections. A 1976 paper prepared by Amory Lovins for the Science Council of Canada covered the period to 2025 and concluded that, given a serious commitment to conservation in Canada, energy demand need not increase significantly at all. Lovins made approximately the same assumptions about population growth and lifestyle as the LEAP study. But he asserted that through vigorous energy conservation, much lower per capita energy consumption was possible, and primary energy consumption in the year 2025 could be as low as 9.4 quads, or approximately half that of the LEAP forecast. He argued further that, with the significant lifestyle changes embodied in the concept of the conserver society, even greater savings would be possible, and final demand could be held to about 5.1 quads, or 36 per cent less in 2025 than in 1975.[8]

Another study that looked at a number of different energy consumption scenarios to the year 2025 was prepared in early 1977 as a background paper for the LEAP report. The paper looked at the growth in secondary energy consumption and concluded that "average annual growth of 2 per cent year for 1975 to 2025 seems to be a better upper limit than 3 per cent. Scenario results centre around 1 per cent per year or a little more."[9] This 2 per cent upper limit in secondary energy consumption would require about 21.5 quads primary energy in 2025; the 1 per cent centre figure yields about 13.2 quads for the same year compared with the LEAP projection of 20 quads. The study considered lower energy growth scenarios to be feasible given a commitment to increased energy efficiency:

> Assuming that we are going to be energy efficient in 2025, it is easier to develop lower growth scenarios than higher ones. This means that secondary energy consumption in 2025 could easily drop to some lower level, not much if at all above today's level, such that the annual rate of growth *per capita* between 1975 and 2025 would remain at zero. This would, of course, be a major shift . . . still lower levels of energy conservation are conceivable. However, to do so would eventually require shifts beyond the economically justified measures now foreseen.[10]

Demand Forecasts and Energy Policy

As time has passed and we have moved into the 1980s, energy demand projections have shrunk. The trend has been towards lower growth projections and greater advocacy of conservation as an important approach to helping solve our energy supply problems. There seem to be two reasons for this.

First, as the economy has had a chance to react to the changes in the energy situation begun in 1973, the rate of energy consumption growth has fallen somewhat. The larger energy demand increases projected earlier in the 1970s have just not occurred. As a result, both our total energy demand and our energy growth rate going into the 1980s are lower than some earlier projections. When forecasting forty years or more into the future, a relatively small change in energy consumption levels and energy demand growth rates assumed for the first years of the projection can make a large difference in the energy consumption levels forecast for the end of the period. Consequently many of the longer range projections made earlier in the decade have had to be revised downward significantly.

Second, and perhaps more important, is the shift from aggregate studies to ones that draw on careful "engineering" examinations of specific conservation possibilities. The more detailed the examination of specific conservation opportunities in each of our energy consuming sectors, the stronger has been the conclusion that important improvements in the efficiency of energy use are possible. So, as time has passed and more conservation opportunities have emerged and been integrated into energy demand projections, the greater has become the acknowledged potential for conservation. Basically these studies have come to the conclusion that a significantly lower level of energy demand growth is possible; they have also concluded that conservation is a much more economical way to "produce" energy than some of the exclusively supply-oriented solutions that have been put forward to close the gap between energy supply and demand.

Two of the most recent and dramatic examples of this trend are studies undertaken in the United States. In 1979 the Harvard Business School's energy project published a report entitled *Energy Future,* which concluded that energy conservation has great potential in the United States and represents that country's most economic option for replacing imported oil. It called for a turnaround in U.S. government policy towards a major commitment to energy conservation programs.[11] Another study, entitled *Energy in Transition,* represents the culmination of a mammoth effort by the U.S. National Academy of Science in assembling information on U.S. energy prospects.[12] Hundreds of experts were involved over a five-year period in exploring future energy supply and demand prospects to the year 2010. Looking at demand, the study concluded that a wide range of possibilities exist, all consistent with current lifestyle and economic growth of 2 per cent in real terms. The "no change" scenario – present policies continued into the future –

19

would result in aggregate U.S. demand of about 135 quads by 2010 or about twice the 1975 demand of 70.8 quads. By contrast, a scenario embodying as aggressive conservation campaign "aimed at maximum efficiency plus some minor lifestyle changes" results in demand of 73.6 quads, just marginally higher than the 1975 level.[13]

What is now acknowledged but has not been generally recognized in the past is that there is a wide range in energy consumption patterns and rates consistent with broadly the same economic and social future as today. The basic difference is the efficiency with which we use energy to deliver the same range of end uses. Another common theme of these studies is that appropriate government policies have to be implemented in order to capture the potential for conservation. Policies are needed in order to overcome a wide range of barriers to conservation and to accelerate and ease the shift to lower growth in energy consumption. The task cannot be left to the workings of the market, for within certain limits energy demand is a matter of political choice. Given political and social will, it is possible that we can opt for a much lower rate of energy consumption growth.

What do these studies suggest for Canada's future energy requirements? First they indicate that energy conservation is a key energy resource and that important gains in energy efficiency can be made. Conservation may be able to play a central role in helping us ease our energy problem. They also suggest that it may not be necessary to lock ourselves into the kind of energy growth we have had in the past in order to sustain and improve our standard of living.

Second, the studies imply that in order to take full advantage of the opportunities offered by energy conservation governments must assume a leadership role. Without government commitment to eliminate many of the barriers currently inhibiting energy conserving practices and without government encouragement of the rapid improvement in the energy efficiency of our current capital stock – for example, through standards and incentives – Canada will experience both a lower level of energy conservation and a much more painful and inequitable adjustment process.

The federal government and some provinces have already taken important initiatives in the conservation area. The Canadian Home Insulation Program and the federal mileage standards for automobiles are instances of this. Unfortunately these remain among a small number of examples. If Canada is to make a serious and effective move to increase conservation, a much more systematic and comprehensive set of initiatives co-ordinated with an overall long-range energy supply plan is necessary. Chapter 6 proposes the best government vehicle for this.

We should not underemphasize the shift in orientation required from our politicians and bureaucrats by a serious commitment to conservation. Government's limited involvement has been almost entirely concerned with matters of energy supply. If past behaviour is a guide to future performance, our political leaders will be more interested in a new pipeline or tar sands plant than they will in announcing decreases in industrial energy consumption. Government has to go beyond lip service to a serious commitment to energy conservation.

Real potential exists to be much more aggressive about energy conservation than we have been to date. At the same time, more detailed, implementation-oriented analyses of conservation possibilities are required. Thoroughgoing studies are needed, particularly to identify that set of measures best suited for reaching an acceptable level of energy conservation. For example, what government incentives, education programmes, and/or standards in combination with what adjustments in energy prices would be most effective, equitable, and least disruptive in reaching our energy conservation goals?

Some assert that the answer to this last question is really quite simple, arguing that the price of energy should be used to determine the desired level of consumption and should serve, if not as the sole, at least as the major basis for conservation. While there is no doubt that higher prices result in some decreased use of energy, what is at issue is both the effectiveness and the equity of the price mechanism compared with other methods in bringing about warranted decreases in energy demand.

The major barrier to lower energy consumption is the energy inefficiency of our existing stock of buildings, automobiles, factories, and appliances. In the short term it is difficult to alter this stock, and frequently such an alteration requires a relatively significant capital outlay. Consequently the response to energy price increases, especially in the short term, often can be curtailment rather than conservation through the increased efficiency that results from improved insulation or changed industrial processes.

In those cases where the energy is a necessity – for example, home heating or automobile trips that simply cannot be avoided – other purchases of goods and services are curtailed in order to accommodate the increase in the outlay for energy. Also, increased energy prices more frequently force those on lower incomes to curtail activities because they cannot afford to make improvements in efficiency that would conserve energy. This heightens the already regressive impact of energy price rises since those on lower and middle incomes already spend proportionately more of their earnings directly on energy than those in higher brackets.

There are therefore, a number of reasons for rejecting price as the primary mechanism for achieving the desired levels of conservation. A price increase is a blunt instrument for reducing energy consumption. The response may be inefficient and fail to bring about a significant decrease in energy use. In addition, inequities in income distribution are exacerbated. Furthermore, energy price increases are highly inflationary, affecting virtually all aspects of the economy with their multiplier effects. Thus price rises must be considered very carefully along with other proposals.

This study advocates a cost-based approach to energy pricing (see Chapter 5). Under this scheme the price would be determined directly by the Canadian costs for oil and gas and for developing other sources of energy required to ensure a sustainable energy base. After a thorough examination of the range of possibilities available for reducing energy demand, prices for various forms of energy would be fixed and modified in light of all the circumstances necessary to bring about satisfactory long-term supply/demand balance. Undoubtedly it will also be advisable to use other mechanisms to allocate the available supplies of those fuels in greatest demand and in short supply.

For example, after due consideration of all the options, rationing of petroleum might seem to be the most satisfactory method for handling problems of high oil and gasoline demand in the period of transition to a sustainable energy base. Gasoline consumption accounted for 38 per cent of both domestic and imported petroleum products used in Canada in 1979. If that consumption could be reduced 25 per cent, the total amount of petroleum used annually would fall by 66 million barrels, or nearly 10 per cent. While such a reduction might be achieved by raising prices, the less advantaged members of society would bear the costs most heavily.

A form of rationing could be adopted to achieve the 25 per cent reduction more equitably. Ration coupons adding up to 75 per cent of present consumption after providing for the additional requirements of farmers, fishermen, and truckers would be issued. Arrangements could be made for those who did not want to use their coupons to sell them to others, possibly through the service stations of the oil companies. Those who required additional quantities of gasoline would have to pay a premium for the extra coupons they would need. Rationing is, of course, frequently dismissed as being an intolerable and unacceptable method, except in short-term emergencies. It is, allegedly, not in keeping with a free-enterprise system. The problems of black markets are highlighted by opponents of rationing as are the abuses experienced during wartime. However, some studies indicate that rationing could be the most effective, equitable, and least disruptive approach to deal with oil shortages.[14] At the very least this alternative deserves close scrutiny.

LEAP and Future Demand

From the preceding discussion it is clear that a wide range of possibilities exists for estimating Canada's long-range energy demand. However, for purposes of examining supply and demand prospects in this study, it is necessary to have some specific reference point. The LEAP scenario provides a convenient point of departure. It is one of the few long-term forecasts of Canadian energy demand, and it systematically considers both the aggregate energy demand patterns of the past and conservation possibilities for the future.[15] This forecast foresees a significant decline in demand growth through active government support. The LEAP demand scenario foresees average annual growth in primary energy demand of 2.8 per cent to the year 2000 and 0.9 per cent from 2000-25. Adoption of this not unreasonable projection allows us to explore energy supply problems in the context of a thoughtfully prepared demand forecast.

Other estimates of conservation potential have suggested a lower growth rate is feasible and appropriate. However, it is clear that lower figures are attainable only if significant effort and commitment are made to vigorous conservation initiatives. Such effort and commitment have yet to materialize, either on the part of the government or society generally. In fact current energy demand growth rates of about 4 per cent are higher than the LEAP report's 2.8 per cent average to 2000, as are the two recent NEB projections.[16] Consequently it would be inadvisable and certainly premature at this point to base an assessment of Canada's supply requirements on even lower forecasts of future primary energy consumption.

However, it should be emphasized that adoption of the LEAP forecast does not necessarily imply advocacy of it. As the previous and following sections make clear, Canada must undertake a serious and active investigation of the feasibility of lowering our energy demand further than the LEAP scenario in concert with a full long-term evaluation of our supply options. Should a lower demand course prove feasible as indeed it must in the long-term – and the studies cited above suggest such a possibility – an aggressive program must be assembled and tenaciously pursued.

Future Demand by Energy Source

The LEAP report, in assessing how energy demand to the year 2025 might be met, appears to have scrutinized the potential availability and cost of the full range of conventional and nonconventional energy forms. On the basis of this evaluation, the report allocated the different portions of total energy demand to the various energy supply possibilities. This breakdown of future energy demand into energy type is set out for the whole 1975–2025 period in Chart 2-1, and for specific years in Table 2-2. This is the allocation by energy type that is adopted as the point of departure for Chapters 3 and 4 of this study.

In the figure in which the respective areas for each form of energy reflect accurately the relative contributions required from each future source of energy supply, the magnitude of the challenge facing industry and governments begins to come into focus. In Table 2-2 the LEAP estimates indicate that renewable solar, wind, and biomass energy will be capable of supplying no more than 5 per cent of demand in 2000 and 10 per cent of requirements in 2025. This leaves 15.2 quads and 18.0 quads to be met by non-renewables, including hydro-electric power, in these years. But, as the LEAP report points out, renewable energy resources excluding hydro will be called upon to supply the energy equivalent of nearly one-quarter of that now supplied by oil by 2000 and to supply more than one-half that equivalence by 2025.[17]

TABLE 2-2
ENERGY DEMAND FORECAST, BY ENERGY SOURCE,
1975–2025

| | | | | Share of market | | |
	1975	2000	2025	1975	2000	2025
	(10^{15} Btus)			(Per cent)		
Petroleum	3.70	4.80	5.00	46	30	25
Natural gas	1.50	3.20	3.60	19	20	18
Electricity						
Coal	0.92	2.16	2.44	11	14	12
Nuclear	0.14	2.38	3.48	2	15	18
Hydro	1.74	2.52	2.63	22	16	13
Other	—	0.14	0.85	—	—	4
Renewables	—	0.80	2.00	—	5	10
Total	8.00	16.00	20.00	100	100	100

Source: J.E. Gander and F.W. Belaire, *Energy Futures for Canadians* (LEAP) (Ottawa: Energy, Mines and Resources Canada, 1978), p. 160.

Hydro power, long the mainstay of electrical generation in Canada, has limited possibilities for major expansion because most readily accessible sites have been developed. New forms of hydro power, such as tidal, wave, or low-head hydraulic, may prove feasible though costly in the future. In this demand forecast, hydro-electric generation is as-

CHART 2-1
ENERGY REQUIREMENTS, BY SOURCE, 1960–2025

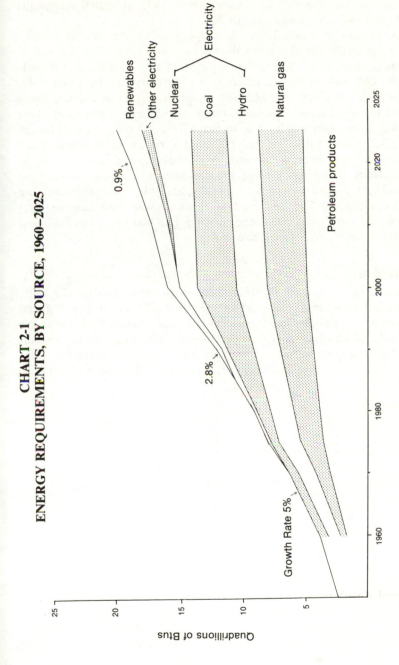

Renewables

Other electricity

Electricity { Nuclear, Coal, Hydro

Natural gas

0.9%

2.8%

Petroleum products

Growth Rate 5%

Quadrillions of Btus

25   20   15   10   5

1960   1980   2000   2020   2025

Source: J.E. Gander and F.W. Belaire, *Energy Futures for Canadians* (LEAP) (Ottawa: Energy, Mines and Resources Canada, 1978), p. 160.

25

sumed to increase from 37,000 megawatts in 1975 to 69,000 megawatts in 2000 and to 72,000 megawatts in 2025.[18]

While petroleum is called upon to supply smaller and smaller percentages of the totals, the absolute volumes increase from 3.7 to 4.8 and to 5.0 quads. These latter figures are equivalent to 630 million, 830 million, and 860 million barrels of crude oil annually for the years 1975, 2000 and 2025, respectively. The percentage share met by natural gas is assumed to stay relatively constant, but in absolute amounts production for domestic markets will have to increase from 1.5 trillion cubic feet in 1975 to 3.2 trillion cubic feet in 2000 and 3.6 trillion cubic feet in 2025. In order to meet energy demand, coal consumption would have to increase from 46 million tons in 1975 to 110 million tons in the year 2000 and 120 million tons in 2025. Finally, assuming the continuing use of a "once-through" Candu nuclear reactor cycle, uranium requirements would grow from 200 tonnes in 1975 to 3,800 tonnes in 2000 and to 5,500 tonnes by 2025 (see Chapter 4).

Conclusion

The overall rate of growth in demand has been cut in half for the 1975-2000 period compared with that of the 1960–75 period and reduced by a further two-thirds – to 0.9 per cent per year – for 2000–25. Still, the magnitude of absolute energy supply needs is formidable to contemplate. The ability of Canada's energy resources to meet these ever, and in some cases rapidly, increasing requirements for energy supply is examined in the next two chapters.

26

The Outlook for Crude Oil and Natural Gas Supplies

3

Today oil is the principal source of energy in Canada, supplying over 40 per cent of our energy requirements.[1] The second largest non-renewable source of energy supply in this country is natural gas.[2] Therefore, an analysis of the anticipated future supply of oil and natural gas is fundamental for any long-term energy study. Where adequate information is available, this analysis focuses on the magnitude of reserves, the rate at which the magnitude is changing as a result of new discoveries or other factors affecting the amounts of recoverable reserves, forecasts of future production rates, and consideration of political factors such as limitations on production that may be imposed by governments. The main purpose of the first section is to determine the extent to which the supplies of conventional crude oil can be relied upon to perform their current function as the primary source of world and domestic energy supply. The second section considers the role of natural gas in the energy equation. Each energy source is examined in the world, United States, and Canadian contexts.

Crude Oil Supplies Worldwide and Domestic

Chart 3-1 presents historical data on the rate at which world oil production increased during the 1930–77 period. Also included is one of the forecasts for future production rates prepared by the Workshop on Alternative Energy Strategies (WAES), a group of seventy people recruited from business, industry, governments, and universities in fifteen major non-communist oil importing countries. In 1977, in its evaluation of oil supply prospects, WAES concluded that if all the oil producing countries outside communist areas allowed production to increase to meet demands, limited only by technical factors, oil production would peak and decline before the end of the century and that this would hold over a wide range of assumptions.[3]

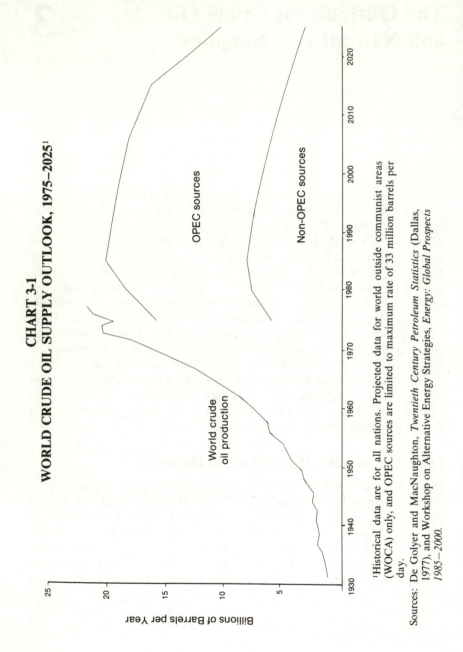

CHART 3-1
WORLD CRUDE OIL SUPPLY OUTLOOK, 1975–2025[1]

OPEC sources

Non-OPEC sources

World crude
oil production

Billions of Barrels per Year

1930　1940　1950　1960　1970　1980　1990　2000　2010　2020

[1]Historical data are for all nations. Projected data for world outside communist areas (WOCA) only, and OPEC sources are limited to maximum rate of 33 million barrels per day.

Sources: De Golyer and MacNaughton, *Twentieth Century Petroleum Statistics* (Dallas, 1977), and Workshop on Alternative Energy Strategies, *Energy: Global Prospects 1985–2000.*

28

Since WAES published its report, the upheavals in Iran and Iraq have confirmed the sensitivity of world oil production to political events in the major producing countries. The ability of the members of the OPEC cartel to raise prices unilaterally has been demonstrated again and again. Recent gasoline shortages in the United States and elsewhere undoubtedly are harbingers of the near future for those countries dependent on imports. Furthermore, a report released by a U.S. Senate subcommittee stated that future output of Saudi Arabian oil will be far lower than expected and that top capacity will not exceed 12 million barrels per day in 1987. This is in contrast to fairly recent predictions that Saudi Arabia could produce 20 million barrels per day by 1980. The report also stated that the Saudis had reduced their estimate of oil remaining in the ground by 71 billion barrels, presumably as a result of recent disappointing exploratory drilling experience and other assessment techniques.[4] In addition, John R. Kiely, chairman, International Executive Council of the World Energy Conference, stated recently that he is now convinced that world oil production has already peaked.[5] On the strength of these reports and developments it is not unreasonable to conclude that the WAES report on future world oil availablility may well be optimistic and that Chart 3-1 probably overstimates the volume of oil that will be available to the oil-importing nations.

The recent large addition to the proved oil reserves of Mexico might have been expected to offset pessimism about world oil supplies. That country – which, although not a member of OPEC, charges "world" or higher prices for exports – now estimates its proved recoverable oil reserves at over 40 billion barrels, compared with only 8 billion barrels two years ago. However, the Mexican government has decided to level off oil production at 2.25 million barrels per day in 1980 to prolong the life of the reserve for nearly fifty years.[6] Since Mexico's own consumption is about 750 thousand barrels per day and rising, a maximum of 1.5 million barrels per day will be available for export. This will not be a highly significant volume in a world that currently consumes 60 million barrels per day.

In view of the outlook for declining world oil supplies and increasing prices, it would be unwise for Canada to continue to rely on oil imports to provide any appreciable amount of the country's vital energy needs. In the past this policy, recommended to the government by the major oil companies, has left Canada highly vulnerable to the inevitable declines in world oil availability and excessive price increases by the OPEC nations. The economic impact of these aspects of national energy policy has already been reflected to some degree in Canada's high rates of inflation and unemployment, which can only worsen unless this flaw in past policy and practice is soon corrected.

29

CHART 3-2
REMAINING PROVED OIL RESERVES, UNITED STATES 1920–78

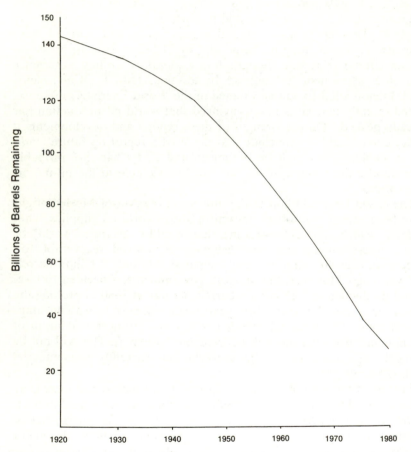

Source: Based on data from U.S. Bureau of Mines, and the American Petroleum
Institute.

United States Crude Oil Supply Outlook
The U.S. domestic oil supply outlook is serious and deteriorating. Chart 3-2 shows the remaining U.S. proved crude oil reserves on a year-by-year basis, assuming that total recoverable reserves will, in fact, turn out to be the sum of cumulative production to date of 118 billion barrels plus the 1978 estimate of remaining recoverable reserves of 29.5 billion barrels. On this basis, 80 per cent of total known recoverable reserves had been produced by 1978. Chart 3-3 plots remaining U.S. proved reserves as calculated annually by the American Petroleum Institute for the 1950–78 period. Year-by-year changes result from adding to the previous year's estimate the reserve additions for the current year then subtracting annual production. These figures also show the relative significance of the Prudhoe Bay discovery, which was treated as a 1970 reserve addition, although it was not connected by

CHART 3-3
PROVED CRUDE OIL RESERVES, UNITED STATES, 1950–78

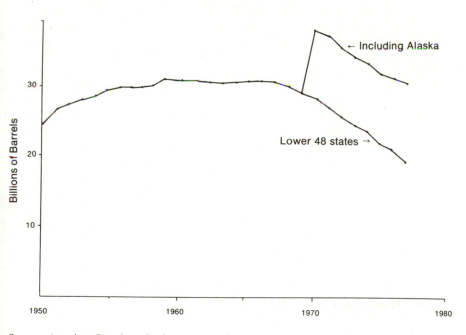

Source: American Petroleum Institute.

31

pipeline until 1977. Total U.S. petroleum demand, which now exceeds 6 billion barrels annually, is met approximately half by domestic production and half by refined and crude oil imports. Imports have increased by 400 per cent since 1960 as demand increased, while domestic reserves remained static and then declined. Thus the rate of decline in proved reserves can properly be described as alarming.

Canada's contribution to U.S. crude oil imports began in 1951 and reached a peak of 365 million barrels in 1973. By 1978 Canadian oil exports had declined to 98 million barrels, or 18 per cent of Canadian production of 525 million barrels.[7] U.S. yearly oil demand of 6.5 billion barrels is now equivalent to more than the total remaining Canadian conventional proved oil reserves of 5.8 billion barrels. There is no way Canada can begin to help solve the U.S. oil shortage problem, although Canada in response to industry pressure in 1979 was continuing to export about 300,000 barrels per day of its dwindling reserves of crude oil and natural gas liquids.[8]

Perhaps of more concern is the fact that it is highly unlikely that future discoveries will significantly improve the conventional oil supply outlook in the United States. According to a report on worldwide oil reserves recently prepared for the U.S. Central Intelligence Agency by the Rand Corporation, exploration techniques employed by industry in recent years have been highly efficient with the result that the great majority of giant and super-giant oil fields have already been discovered.[9] This suggests that the possibility of discovering new large oil fields in the United States is remote. And, indeed, apart from the Prudhoe Bay discovery in 1968, there have been no noteworthy new oil finds in the United States during the past twenty years.

Similarly, according to the Rand report, the potential for significant reserve additions from extensions to known fields, while important in the past, will not be large in the future and will occur within three to five years of the drilling of the discovery well. In recent years, because of oil shortages, the boundaries of new finds have been delineated and production wells drilled much more rapidly than in the past. The report concluded that the "appreciation" of earlier discoveries, hitherto a significant contributor to reserve growth, will not be of major consequence in the future.

Based on these conclusions Chart 3-2 will likely prove to be a fairly accurate portrayal of the ultimate quantity of recoverable U.S. conventional oil reserves. The annual rate of producibility from known domestic reserves will decline with time and the need for imports will increase if the U.S. economy and living standards are to be maintained at anywhere near their present level.

32

CHART 3-4
PROVED CONVENTIONAL CRUDE OIL RESERVES, CANADA, 1950–78

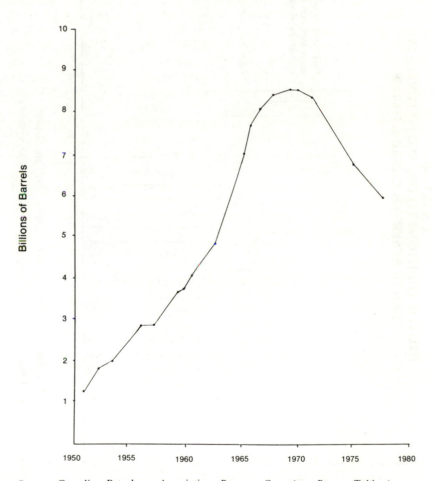

Source: Canadian Petroleum Association, *Reserves Committee Report*, Table 4.

33

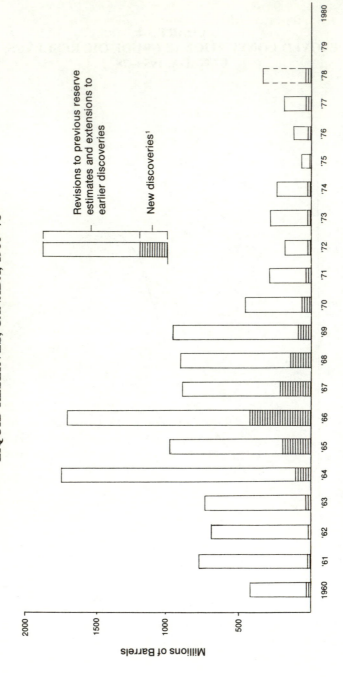

CHART 3-5
PROVED ADDITIONS TO OIL AND NATURAL GAS
LIQUID RESERVES, CANADA, 1960–78

Revisions to previous reserve
estimates and extensions to
earlier discoveries

New discoveries[1]

Millions of Barrels

[1] Except for 1978 which is proved plus "probable", now termed "established".

Source: Based on data from Canadian Petroleum Association Reserves Committee reports.

34

Canadian Conventional Oil Supply Outlook

Canada's conventional crude oil reserves are not large by international standards, representing only 1.14 per cent of the world total in January 1977.[10] Pembina, the largest Canadian oil field estimated originally to have contained a total of about 1.4 billion barrels recoverable, is now more than 60 per cent depleted.[11] On the basis of its original reserves, it ranks 68th in the world in size.[12] Canadian reserves rose rapidly during the 1950s and 1960s, peaked in 1969, and declined by about 35 per cent during the 1970s. With demand continuing to increase throughout the 1970s, the ratios of reserves to production and reserves to consumption have fallen even faster.[13] Chart 3-4 plots year-by-year proved crude oil reserves, showing that oil reserves are declining rapidly.

Chart 3-5 shows annual gross additions to reserves for crude oil and natural gas liquids, which are the volatile liquid hydrocarbons associated with production and refining of oil and production of natural gas, including liquid petroleum gases (LPGs) such as propane and butane. The chart breaks down reserve additions to those resulting from new discoveries and those brought about by revisions of previous estimates and extensions to earlier discoveries for the 1960–78 period and shows clearly the rapid drop-off in reserves additions that occurred in the 1970s. It also demonstrates the modest level of new discoveries during the past decade, which includes the highly publicized West Pembina find. The potential of frontier areas – East coast offshore, High Eastern Arctic, and Mackenzie Delta-Beaufort Sea – for commercial oil deposits is, according to the National Energy Board, too speculative to predict possible supply contributions.[14] Recent lack of industry response to bidding for Arctic offshore petroleum rights offered by the federal government suggests that these areas may hold little significant prospect for commercial reserves, despite statements by industry spokesmen to the contrary.

Chart 3-6 illustrates the life index of proved crude oil reserves against the wellhead price for crude oil for the period up to 1979. The life index is the theoretical number of years the reserves would last if produced continuously at the current average rate. The ratio is useful because it takes into account two principal variables: the magnitude of reserves, and the rate of production. From the figure it can be seen that while the Canadian government embarked on its "high-price scenario" in the mid-1970s in an effort to slow growth in demand and bring on much needed new supplies, that policy has not had the latter effect and it is debatable how well it has done the former. Despite oil industry promises and government hopes, the Canadian consumer has been paying a high price for domestic crude without any improvement in the

35

CHART 3-6
LIFE INDEX FOR CRUDE OIL, CANADA, 1960–78

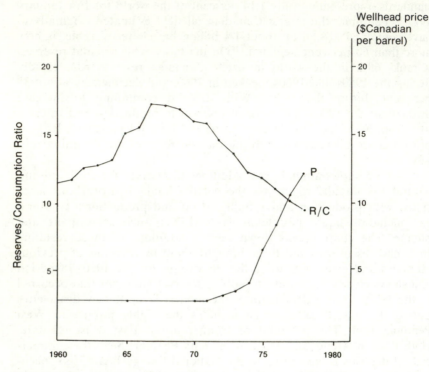

Source: Based on data from Canadian Petroleum Association, *Oilweek*, and oil industry reports.

supply outlook. Secure supplies have continued to deteriorate rapidly throughout the 1970s and are now dangerously low.

Forecast of Future Canadian Oil Availability

In September 1978, following extensive public hearings held across Canada, the National Energy Board published a comprehensive report analysing the Canadian total demand for energy and refined petroleum products and the supply of conventional crude oil, natural gas liquids (NGLs), and industry's plans for synthetic oil from the Athabasca Tar Sands and heavy oil projects.[15] The document projected both demand and supply over the seventeen-year period from 1978 to 1995 and considered export volumes, oil ports of entry, and national pipeline facilities.

Chart 3-7 shows the NEB forecasts for petroleum supply from existing and presently proposed new sources for the 1978–95 period. Forecast supply is projected to the year 2025 to coincide with the time period of the LEAP demand forecast. LEAP predicts that oil requirements will rise from 630 million barrels in 1975 to 830 million barrels in 2000 and to 860 million barrels in 2025. Under this projection, oil would supply a declining percentage of Canada's total energy needs, dropping from about 45 per cent currently to 30 per cent by 2000 and to 25 per cent by 2025. The NEB oil demand forecast exceeds that of the LEAP report by about 6 per cent, even though the NEB projects average annual growth in demand for petroleum products of only 1.4 per cent, a rate that was exceeded by a considerable margin in 1979. Indeed, according to the NEB's 1979 Annual Report, petroleum consumption in Canada has increased at an average growth rate of 4.8 per cent during the 1975–79 period. LEAP assumes a significant substitution of natural gas for fuel oil in the residential heating market and that the more difficult substitutions for oil in the transportation and industrial markets will be tackled with some success.

Chart 3-7 also shows dramatically the rate at which petroleum demand increased in the 1960s and the early 1970s and demonstrates the even more rapid rate at which the oil industry increased productive capacity between 1960 and 1973, selling to both domestic and export markets. It further indicates the alarmingly steep rate at which the producibility of established reserves of crude oil and NGLs is expected to decline in the future. This curve is the NEB's judgment of the falling deliverability of all presently producing oil and NGL sources, after hearing representations from the operators of the individual pools and fields. However, in April 1979 the NEB was reported to have discovered that western Canadian oilfields were not capable of producing as much oil as had been forecast only a few months earlier. This suggests that the position of the lowest curve on this figure may be too high.[16] If this is the case, the other projections are similarly optimistic, and the supply deficit will likely be even larger than indicated here.

The annual production of the Great Canadian Oil Sands (GCOS) – now Suncor – and Syncrude plants, both of which are assumed to have thirty-year producing lives, is expected to be 220,000 barrels per day by 1985. Production from reserves additions is projected to come from new discoveries and enhanced recoveries from existing fields. If these fail to materialize, total supply will once again have been overstated. If, however, there is a better-than-anticipated finding rate, an improvement in this picture would result. However, since no major oil fields have been discovered in the past fifteen years and therefore limited possibilities exist for reserves "appreciation", the likelihood of overstatement would appear to be greater than for possible improvement.

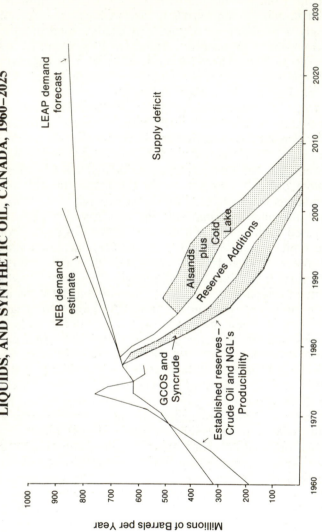

CHART 3-7
DEMAND FOR AND SUPPLY OF CRUDE OIL, NATURAL GAS LIQUIDS, AND SYNTHETIC OIL, CANADA, 1960–2025

Millions of Barrels per Year

LEAP demand forecast

NEB demand estimate

Supply deficit

Alsands plus Cold Lake

Reserves Additions

GCOS and Syncrude

Established reserves — Crude Oil and NGL's Producibility

Sources: Based on data from J.E. Gander and F.W. Belaire, *Energy Futures for Canadians* (LEAP) (Ottawa: Energy, Mines and Resources Canada, 1978), National Energy Board, *Oil Report* (Ottawa, 1978); Shell Canada, *Annual Report, 1978.*

38

The area shown as "Alsands plus Cold Lake" was derived by assuming that projects currently being studied by Shell Canada Limited and Imperial Oil Limited do, in fact, proceed. Shell is project manager for a nine-member consortium that proposes a 140 thousand barrels per day synthetic crude mining and bitumen upgrading facility in the Athabasca Tar Sands of Alberta. Shell has indicated dissatisfaction with existing price and taxation regimes and has stated that it will proceed only if governments grant the project tax, pricing, and royalty arrangements satisfactory to the participating companies. Imperial's Cold Lake project would produce and upgrade 140 thousand barrels per day of viscous heavy oil from deposits located 200 miles northeast of Edmonton. The company is reported to be looking for other corporate entities to join it to the extent of 50 per cent of the equity and has indicated that the project will not go forward unless governments come up with more "incentives" for the company.[17] For purposes of this analysis these projects are assumed to be viable, proceeding on schedules that would have them reaching full production by mid-1986, though neither project is now on its original schedule. Together they would produce 102 million barrels per year, perhaps an optimistic rate. Both projects require Alberta approvals that are not automatic. In 1979, each project was stated to cost between $4 and $5 billion in current dollars.

The most striking aspect of Chart 3-7 is the small magnitude of assured future production compared with Canada's forecast petroleum needs, even though the possible level of future oil requirements has been held down. When this is coupled with the realization that because of reserve inadequacies and pipeline capacity limitations, Canada in 1979 was already importing one-third of its daily requirements of 1.9 million barrels while continuing to export 300 thousand barrels per day, the degree of the nation's oil supply weakness and vulnerability comes into focus.

As mentioned, Chart 3-7 portrays the NEB's estimate of reserves additions it expects from new oilfield discoveries and enhanced recovery schemes in older pools. However, the Chart does not provide any forecast of future production that might come from the highly publicized frontier areas. The reasons for this are twofold.

First, the NEB *Oil Report* concluded, after hearing the representations of eleven industry and government entities, that "it would be too speculative to adopt a potential estimate for these areas at this time, or to attempt to predict reserves additions for the forecast period."[18] The report noted that commercial quantities of oil have not been found in any of the frontier areas, although discoveries had been recorded in four of them. Even the most enthusiastic of the frontier operators, Dome Petroleum Limited, had declined to submit to the NEB any estimates of current and potential reserves. Imperial Oil Limited's submission stated that because of poorer-than-expected exploration results during the previous two years in the Arctic Islands and the Beaufort-Mackenzie Delta areas, it had downgraded its estimates for potential oil supply from these regions.

Second, the results of exploratory drilling since the NEB report, while encouraging, are far too limited for even partially reliable estimates to be made of the magnitude of possible recoverable reserves. Only after reserves have been quantified can the economics of hoped-for production be calculated to determine whether a particular pool is commercial or not. Drillstem tests on a single well provide no information on the likely productive area of a geological structure and hence the amount of oil that may be in place. Only further drilling can establish the extent of a pool.

In both the Hibernia and Beaufort Sea areas additional drilling was undertaken in 1980, but the pace is so slow and the environmental hazards so severe that it will likely be years before dependable reserves estimates leading to reliable evaluations are possible. In the meantime, conventional oil reserves in the Southern Basin can be expected to dwindle and production fall off along the path illustrated. Also, it can be expected that there will be much stock market activity accompanying exploration rumors and company news releases but these should not be permitted to frustrate or impede the development of sound national energy planning and policy.

Unquestionably the possibility exists that the existence of commercial-sized reserves in the frontier areas can result in an improvement in the oil supply outlook portrayed in Chart 3-7. However, it should not be taken for granted that their mere existence is synonomous with future oil availability. To achieve reliable and environmentally safe production will require the construction and operation of complex gathering and transportation systems capable of withstanding the powerful forces of nature. The realities of this challenge and whether practical and economic engineering solutions are even possible have not yet been confronted, let alone surmounted in the Beaufort Sea region. Production problems off Newfoundland have been likened to those of the North Sea except for the presence of icebergs.

It is impossible at this stage to forecast whether the Beaufort Sea and offshore Newfoundland areas will prove to be future sources of oil supply for Canada. However, as will be noted in Chapter 5, guesses about the possible magnitude of the recoverable reserves in the Hibernia structure suggest that if commercial, it could represent the equivalent of a three- to twelve-month supply for Canada at present rates of consumption. Therefore it would not make much of a reduction in the size of the supply deficit as depicted in Chart 3-7.

Another vivid feature of Chart 3-7 is the manner in which the oil industry rapidly expanded producing rates in the 1960s and early 1970s, thereby shortening the life of the Canadian reserves discovered in the 1940s and 1950s. A substantial portion of this increased production was exported to the United States, even though it must have been obvious to the industry that such exports would undermine the future availability of domestic oil for Canadians. In doing so the industry acted in Canada in a fashion similar to the way it behaved in Libya and Venezuela, where oil reserves were swiftly exploited until those countries somewhat belatedly took charge of the management of their own resources by nationalizing the industry. Today's situation is a serious one for an energy-dependent nation such as Canada. As the figures demonstrate, the time is long past due for strong action to be taken to try and correct the rapidly degenerating outlook.

Natural Gas Supply Worldwide and Domestic

Natural gas is a quite different commodity from crude oil when it comes to world trade because it is not readily transported overseas. While it can be supercooled to a liquid state and carried in liquified natural gas (LNG) tankers, the process is expensive, energy intensive, and potentially very hazardous. Some international LNG trade is carried on today, but it is minor relative to that of crude oil; in 1978, for example, only 3 per cent of the world's gas production ended up as LNG. Recently U.S. regulatory authorities vetoed a project to bring Algerian LNG to the east coast because of high costs and possible political instability in the African supplier nation.

Table 3-1 shows estimated proved world reserves of natural gas in 1977. The United States, with only 9.6 per cent of the world's proved reserves, accounted for 38 per cent of production. Because of its imports from Canada, U.S. consumption is an even larger percentage of the world's total. Canada, with 2.6 per cent of the reserves, reported 5.8 per cent of production. Obviously, both countries are producing at considerably higher than world average rates; this means their reserves will be exhausted first. The table also indicates the considerable share of the U.S.S.R., which delivers some of its natural gas to West Germany and Italy. Some other European nations are concerned about the possible political ramifications of becoming energy dependent on the Soviet Union and have shied away from purchasing Russian natural gas.

41

TABLE 3-1
PROVED RESERVES OF NATURAL GAS, BY COUNTRY, 1977

	Estimated reserves (Trillions of cubic feet)	Share of world total (Per cent)	Flared and marketed production, 1975 (Trillions of cubic feet)	Share of total (Per cent)
North America	294.8	13.15	24.1	44.8
Canada	58.3	2.60	3.1	5.8
United States	216.0	9.63	20.2	37.6
South America	74.7	3.33	1.6	3.0
Europe	161.7	7.22	8.0	14.9
U.S.S.R.	781.0	34.83	10.8	20.1
Africa	208.4	9.30	1.9	3.5
Middle East	603.8	26.95	4.8	8.9
Far East	82.2	3.67	2.4	4.4
Australia-New Zealand	34.7	1.55	0.2	0.4
Totals	2,241.3	100.00	53.8	100.0

Source: DeGolyer and MacNaughton, *Twentieth Century Petroleum Statistics* (Dallas, 1977), p. 16.

The problem confronting us today is that past North American practice has been to exploit resources as soon as possible after they have been discovered, regardless of future considerations. This will exhaust the continent's non-renewable resources prematurely, leave the United States and Canada to depend on imports, if supplies are available, at whatever the price demanded by the nation with reserves to sell.

Natural Gas Supply in the United States

The growth in the natural gas industry in the United States following the Second World War was phenomenal. Marketed production rose from 3.9 trillion cubic feet (Tcf) in 1945 to 22.6 Tcf in 1973 before dropping to 19.3 Tcf in 1978 as a result of heavy production and declining deliverability.[19] The American gas industry, in keeping with prevailing business practice, pursued an enthusiastic sales policy, all the while ignoring the clear warning signs demonstrated by declining life indices.

The competitiveness of natural gas in the marketplace was enhanced by a 1954 decision of the U.S. Supreme Court declaring that the wellhead price of natural gas flowing in interstate commerce must be regulated by federal authorities.[20] The effect was to limit price increases. Under regulation, economies of scale were passed along to the consumer. In spite of the efforts of the powerful petroleum lobby, average wellhead prices rose only from 10.4 cents per thousand cubic feet (Mcf) in 1955 to 17.1 cents per Mcf in 1970. Average consumer rates increased from 51.8 cents per Mcf to 64.1 cents per Mcf during the same interval.[21] With this type of price stability, the the use of natural gas for residential, commercial, and industrial purposes accelerated.

The finite nature of conventional natural gas reserves has now caught up with the industry. Chart 3-8 illustrates how year-end proved reserves rose and then fell during the 1950–77 period.

Recoverable reserves peaked in 1967 at 293 Tcf and, despite the addition of 32 Tcf of Alaskan gas in 1970, declined to 209 Tcf by January 1978 and to 200 Tcf by January 1979. Only 167 Tcf of reserves were connected to pipeline systems at the beginning of 1979 because the Alaska Highway gas pipeline has not been constructed. However, American pipeline companies had been successful in tapping sizable Canadian reserves as well. Whether the Prudhoe Bay reserves will ever be brought south remains an open question. It is doubtful that the proposed $23 billion pipeline can be financed as a private sector project, and both the Canadian and U.S. governments have stated they will not lend their financial support by guaranteeing the pipeline company's debt securities. However, in July 1980 at the urging of the

CHART 3-8
PROVED RESERVES NATURAL GAS, UNITED STATES, 1950–77

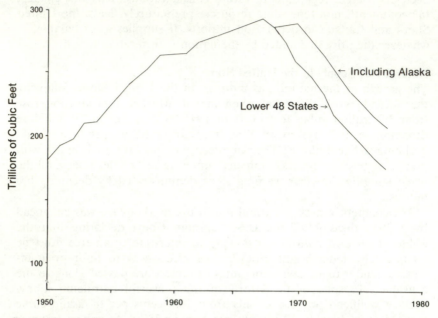

Source: Based on data from American Gas Association, *Gas Facts, 1977* (Arlington, Va., 1978).

Canadian government, the U.S. Congress approved a resolution stating that the pipeline project "enjoys the highest level of Congressional support". But such a resolution is essentially meaningless and does not alter existing law.

Because of the importance of energy to the economic health of the nation and the experiences of the past, the U.S. natural gas industry is closely regulated from wellhead to burnertip by federal and state authorities. As a result of serious supply shortages – the most severe of which occurred during the winter of 1976-77 in the northeastern states – a system of priorities has been established for serving various classes of customers according to end use. The highest priority goes to residential consumers, primarily for wintertime space heating, while the lowest priority has been assigned to large industrial users where alternate fuels are available, including those gas fuelled boilers used in electric generation.

Still, of the total 1977 marketed production of 19.4 Tcf, only 5.0 Tcf were used for high-priority residential purposes – space and water heating, cooking, and air conditioning.[22] The balance went to commercial and industrial accounts of varying size as well as to direct sales by producers for petrochemical usage. Exports from Canada added 1.0 Tcf to total supply, or about 5 per cent of all U.S. consumption. Because of the U.S. system of allocating domestic production in accordance with a ranking of priorities, the additional gas available from Canada increases the total supply and, by displacement, ends up serving the lowest priority market. This is obviously not the best use for a Canadian energy form that will inevitably be in very short supply in the decades ahead.

A total of 3.3 Tcf of natural gas was consumed in 1978 for electric generation.[23] Despite efforts by the U.S. administration to require owners of thermal generating stations to convert from gas to other fuels – primarily coal – this low-priority application of precious natural gas continues. Such extensive use of a diminishing resource for an inefficient energy-conversion process further weakens the U.S. gas supply outlook.

CHART 3-9
LIFE INDEX, NATURAL GAS, UNITED STATES, 1960–77

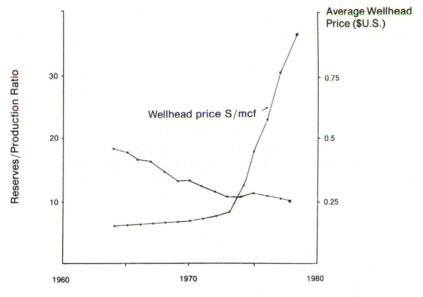

Source: American Gas Association, *Gas Facts, 1977* (Arlington, Va., 1978). Tables 2, 95.

The life index curve for U.S. natural gas, including Alaskan reserves, illustrates the steady decline in the index throughout the 1960s and 1970s (Chart 3-9). A slight rise in the index – from 11.1 to 11.6 – occurred in 1975 when production dropped more rapidly than reserves. Apart from this anomaly, the decline has been quite uniform. Reported year-end proved reserves in the lower forty-eight states have fallen during each of the past eleven years. Also plotted in Chart 3-9 is the average wellhead price of all gas produced for both interstate and intrastate markets.[24] When supplies tightened in the early 1970s, prices began to rise as producers argued successfully for greater "incentives." Average U.S. prices reached 78 cents per Mcf in 1977, a big increase from earlier years but well below the Alberta price of $1.30 for that year. However, as with oil, high prices have not resulted in an improved supply out-look; indeed, the opposite is true. The decline in year-end reserves appears to be unyielding and largely unaffected by price increases. At the same time, high energy costs have had a serious inflationary impact on the U.S. economy and dampened economic growth. There are many lessons for Canada in the U.S. experience.

Natural Gas Supply Outlook in Canada
Although natural gas has been used as an energy source in Canada since the 1890s, the major growth in the Canadian natural gas industry took place after 1955 when the Westcoast Transmission and Trans Canada Pipe Lines systems were constructed. Today natural gas supplies a somewhat smaller percentage of total energy needs in Canada than in the United States for several reasons. The post-Second World War development of long-distance pipelines was about ten years later in Canada and national market development lagged. Natural gas had difficulty penetrating Quebec and other eastern Canada markets because of cost and fear of explosions, the latter triggered by a few unfortunate incidents. The rapid growth in Canadian natural gas markets in the 1960s and early 1970s was cut short by real and apprehended domestic supply shortages from 1973 onwards. Large-scale gas exports to the United States from 1960 onwards limited the supplies available to meet expanding domestic markets. Huge wellhead price increases in 1973 and subsequently rendered natural gas much less competitive vis-a-vis other fuels. A decline in new discoveries since the mid-1960s limited the amounts of natural gas available for both domestic and export markets. And a 1973–74 embargo by Alberta for additional deliveries to central Canada also caused market growth to lose momentum. The net result is that today natural gas supplies a substantially smaller segment of the total energy market in Canada than it did in the U.S. at its peak. Conversely, the potential for market growth for

natural gas in Canada is large if prices and costs are kept within reason and supplies are adequate.

As a result of industry and government declarations, a general impression has been created in Canada that this country possesses substantial surpluses of natural gas for its future needs. Statements by industry spokesmen give the appearance that reserves growth rates have been rapid and that Canadian exports of natural gas to the U.S. should be increased. Industry's efforts have been so convincing that in December 1979 the federal government authorized the export of an additional 3.75 Tcf over the next eight years, representing an increase in the present rate of exports of about 40 per cent. And in February 1980, Pan-Alberta Gas Limited, a subsidiary of Alberta Gas Trunk Line Co. Ltd., applied for still more gas export volumes. In July 1980 the federal government approved the export of these additional volumes along with the "pre-build" export pipeline, despite the absence of firm contractual guarantees from U.S. customers and governments.

Unfortunately, there is a wide discrepancy between the impression of "surplus" and reality. The growth in proved remaining natural gas reserves in Canada as given by statistics prepared by the Canadian Petroleum Association is shown in Chart 3-10 for both the Southern Basin up to 60th parallel plus southern Yukon and NWT, and the Southern Basin plus Mackenzie Delta areas. Without the inclusion of Delta reserves – a questionable addition because of unknown economics – total Canadian proved reserves at the end of 1977 were slightly lower than they were at the end of 1971. Including the Delta, total proved reserves at the beginning of 1978 were estimated at 59.5 Tcf, a modest 7 per cent higher than six years earlier. Southern Basin reserves grew at a generally uniform rate until 1971. In the 1960s, while new discoveries fell off, reserve additions resulting from "appreciation" of earlier finds continued. The rate of growth declined drastically after 1971.

During the 1970s, the industry booked substantial gas reserves additions as a result of inclusion in the recoverable category for the first time of large volumes of shallow low-pressure gas that had long been known to exist but had been considered uneconomic to produce at pre-1973 prices. Despite this inclusion of generally poor quality reserves and the impetus of a tenfold price increase, overall growth in gas reserves has been minimal to nonexistent in the 1970s.

While the CPA does not report gas reserves estimates on a field-by-field basis, it is obvious that depletion of reserves in the larger fields discovered prior to 1965 has offset reserves additions from new finds plus revisions to previous estimates. Indeed, despite the considerable publicity of the industry's exploration activities, it appears that no

CHART 3-10
PROVED NATURAL GAS RESERVES, CANADA, 1950–78

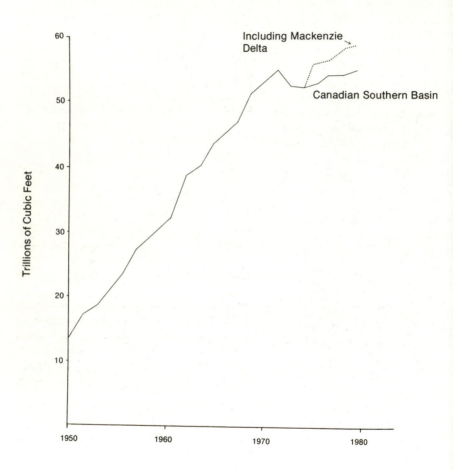

Source: Based on data from the Canadian Petroleum Association.

major new gas fields have been discovered in the Southern Basin for at least the past ten years. Nor, judging by U.S. experience, is it likely that large new oil and gas fields will be discovered in the areas now supplying Canadian domestic and export markets.[25] Further, the reserves of the Mackenzie Delta after more than ten years of exploratory effort have remained relatively small. Clearly exploration and development are in a mature phase in western Canada for both conventional oil and gas.

A further indication of the state of affairs is the decline in natural gas reserves controlled by the industry. Imperial Oil Limited reported in 1979 that its gross proved reserves in the Southern Basin decreased from 3.34 Tcf in 1969 to 2.17 Tcf in 1978, a net reduction of 35 per cent in nine years.[26] Reserves of another significant and highly successful gas producer, Hudson's Bay Oil and Gas Company Limited, dropped by 10 per cent during the 1969–78 period from 3.79 Tcf to 3.41 Tcf.[27]

Chart 3-11 presents the trend in Canadian natural gas life indices for the 1964–77 period. To yield the highest and most optimistic outlook, individual indices were calculated using CPA's "probable" reserves rather than "proved" reserves. The shape of the curve for "proved" reserves is basically the same but about 10 per cent lower. In other words, during this interval, CPA's estimates of "probable" reserves (which includes proved) was about 10 per cent higher than "proved" only. In both cases the ratio drops rather steeply in the 1960s but slackens somewhat in the 1970s while still maintaining the overall downward trend. This indicates an ever-declining level of supply protection from economic sources.

The analysis of trends in the growth of natural gas reserves has been made more difficult by CPA's 1978 decision to discontinue publishing its data on "proved" reserves even though this has been the traditional standard for industry reporting in both the U.S. and Canada for decades. CPA now includes in its gas reserves figures estimates for northern frontier discoveries even though such discoveries have not been established as economic.

Also plotted on Chart 3-11 is the average wellhead price paid for natural gas produced in Alberta during this period. By the fall of 1980, the price had moved up substantially from that shown. The two slight increases in the life index in 1975 and 1977 result in part from decreases in net production as markets shrunk marginally in those years. Existing export customers have failed to buy their full license allotments in recent years, partly as a result of the high price of Canadian gas. This has had the effect of lowering total production somewhat and

CHART 3-11
LIFE INDEX, NATURAL GAS, CANADA, 1964–77

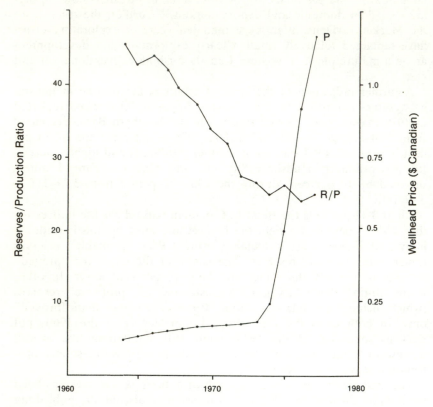

Source: Based on data from the Canadian Petroleum Association and Trans Canada
Pipe Lines, *Annual Report, 1977.*

making the resulting reserve life indices a bit larger. But the huge price
increases agreed upon by the federal and Alberta governments since
1973 have had essentially no impact in improving the gas supply outlook or reversing the downward trend.

The total effect is disquieting to say the least. Natural gas is now
alleged to be Canada's largest future source of energy supply. While
the Canadian life index is presently about double that of the United
States, the trend in both countries is unrelentingly downward, and the
rate of decline in Canada is much steeper than that south of the
border. Price increases have been ineffective in reversing the slide. This

trend, coupled with continuing pressure from the producing industry for increased exports, inevitably will lead to serious future shortages and still higher prices unless strong measures are taken by Canadian authorities to control events and protect the national interest. To accept the industry's arguments that high prices will bring on energy self-sufficiency is to ignore the experience of the past twenty years and to penalize Canadian consumers to the sum of billions of dollars for the benefit of a largely foreign-controlled industry.

Projections of Future Canadian Gas Supply

Two recent analyses of the anticipated ability of Canadian gas reserves to meet the future needs of domestic and currently served export markets have been carried out by Alberta and federal regulatory authorities. After looking briefly at the Alberta study, the discussion focuses on the work done by the National Energy Board.

In May 1978 the Alberta Energy Resources Conservation Board (AERCB) issued its report entitled *The Supply of and Demand for Alberta Gas.*[28] While the Alberta boards' jurisdiction is provincial, this particular analysis dealt not only with Alberta's present and anticipated future gas reserves, but also with those of other provinces. The purpose of the study was to estimate how long Alberta's gas reserves would be able to supply all of Canada's forecast natural gas needs plus previously committed exports. Two separate cases were calculated: one assumed that Alberta's recoverable gas reserves ultimately would total 110 trillion cubic feet; the second, that the ultimate recoverable reserves of the province would total 130 Tcf.

On the basis of the 110 Tcf case, the AERCB's then best judgment of the ultimate gas potential, the AERCB calculated that Alberta's reserves would be able to meet the needs of the provinces east of Alberta only until 1985 when the anticipated decline in gas producibility plus Alberta's thirty-year protection formula for its own provincial needs would begin to limit the volumes of gas that could be made available to the rest of Canada (Chart 3-12). A projection of the data indicates that by 2000 there would be no gas from Alberta to supply the needs of the other provinces.

The results from the 130 Tcf case were somewhat better for the medium term but no real improvement in the longer term (Chart 3-13). The year when Alberta would have to begin limiting the flow of gas to other parts of Canada moved from 1985 to 1992. However, the calculated drop in anticipated supply was steeper. A projection of this forecast supply also indicated that by 2000 there would be no gas for delivery to provinces east of Alberta.

51

52

CHART 3-12
CANADIAN NATURAL GAS PRODUCIBILITY ASSUMING ALBERTA RECOVERABLE RESERVES, OF 110 Tcf, 1977–2000

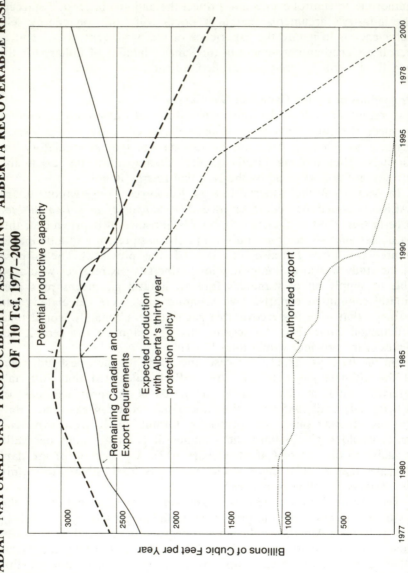

Source: AERCB. *The Supply of and Demand for Alberta Gas* (Calgary, 1978), Figure 8 projected to 2000.

CHART 3-13

CANADIAN NATURAL GAS PRODUCIBILITY ASSUMING ALBERTA RECOVERABLE RESERVES, OF 130 Tcf, 1977–2000

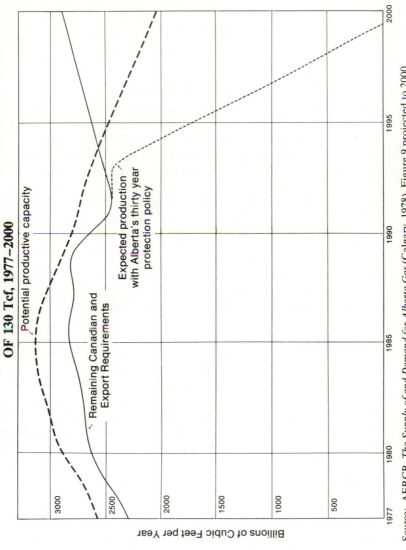

Source: AERCB. *The Supply of and Demand for Alberta Gas* (Calgary, 1978), Figure 9 projected to 2000.

53

The dismaying aspect of the AERCB study is that relatively few years remain until declining deliverability from gas fields discovered in earlier years, coupled with Alberta's own protection formula, will result in gas shortages for the rest of Canada and that almost no supplies will be available by the end of this century. Still, while the producing industry presses successfully for greater exports to the United States and argues strenuously that discovery rates will improve, the indisputable evidence is that awesome gas supply deficiencies are rapidly approaching.

The NEB report, *Canadian Natural Gas Supply and Requirements*, on Canadian natural gas supply and requirements to 2000 was published in February 1979, following extensive public hearings the previous year.[29] The hearing had been called by the Board for a variety of reasons and in anticipation of receiving specific applications from industry to export to the United States additional volumes of natural gas over and above the 10.5 Tcf already approved and remaining to be removed under existing licenses.

The NEB approaches the question of an exportable gas surplus on an arithmetic basis. It estimates reserves, forecasts rates of reserves additions, predicts market requirements and deducts them from anticipated supplies, and determines whether an excess or deficit results. Whether an excess of supply over immediate domestic needs is "surplus to the reasonably foreseeable requirements for use in Canada," the standard set forth in the NEB statute, is a judgment the Board makes after having "regard to all considerations that appear to it to be relevant."[30] Traditionally, the NEB has relied on an arbitrary mathematical formula to reach its findings.

Canadian Natural Gas Supply and Requirements is no exception. Partly by estimating future Canadian requirements at a level about 10 per cent lower than its forecast of eighteen months earlier, the NEB concluded that Canada had an exportable surplus. However, the NEB only managed to reach the conclusion by changing its previous reserves test, which theoretically had been designed to protect Canadian needs. By adding two deliverability "tests" to its weakened reserves "test," the NEB concluded that Canada had an exportable "surplus" of some 2 trillion cubic feet out of total reserves of 66.1 Tcf.

The first deliverability test examines whether Canadian natural gas needs can be met from presently known reserves for a period of five years. The second test, which assumes a generous rate of reserves additions in the Southern Basin during the next decade, calculates a theoretical supply/demand balance assuming reserves additions are actually achieved at this rate. This test is supposed to ensure that Canadian requirements will be fully met for a ten-year period. In view of

54

the grave outlook for crude oil supply and the vital importance of energy, theoretical five and ten-year protection periods for natural gas in Canadian markets are slim indeed. This is particularly true when the experiences of the past decade are taken into account. Using its former reserves protection formula of "25A4" – twenty-five times the Canadian market needs four years hence – the Board approved major new exports in 1970. Within four years there was a serious gas supply shortage in Canada because reserves additions did not come up to expectations. Indeed, as Chart 3-10 demonstrated there was an actual decline in this interval despite producer assurances that the reverse would happen.

Now the NEB has reduced the level of reserves protection to 25A1 – twenty-five times the current level of Canadian use.[31] The change is signficant and obviously adverse to the interests of Canadians dependent on natural gas while, at the same time, benefitting producers. The clear result will be an increase in gas exports, an acceleration of the timing of shortages of growing magnitude, and more rapid price increases costing consumers billions of dollars.

The problems in domestic natural gas supply that lie ahead are readily apparent when the NEB's February 1979 forecast of future gas availability is plotted against the LEAP estimate of anticipated Canadian requirements. Chart 3-14 plots gas producibility calculations carried out by the NEB for presently known reserves plus those for gas assumed to be discovered and developed in the Southern Basin in future years. To this Southern Basin supply forecast is added 260 billion cubic feet (bcf) per year from the Mackenzie Delta projected, for this purpose, to commence flowing in 1994. The magnitude of the predicted future supply deficit is that area between the LEAP requirements estimate and the NEB supply curves.

When both the NEB and LEAP estimates of future demand to 2000 are examined, the NEB forecast is about 12 per cent higher than that of LEAP for the year 2000. While the LEAP report arbitrarily lowered the portion of Canada's total energy requirements to be supplied by natural gas from 20 to 18 per cent, natural gas needs for the year 2025 are still forecast to be 3.6 Tcf, or double today's requirement. When the predicted rate of exhaustion of current producibility is recognized, the likelihood of meeting demands of this magnitude appears remote indeed.

Chart 3-14 also illustrates clearly the rapid rate at which gas production in Canada has grown during the 1960-77 period. The Canadian gas market expanded at a fast pace during the same interval but at a slower rate than production increases. The excess of production over domestic demand has been exported to the United States under licenses issued by the NEB, with the final license due to expire in 1995.[32]

The large proportion of Canadian reserves dedicated to exports relative to that for Canadian use is readily apparent in this figure.

Whether the sizable estimate of the NEB for future reserve additions will actually materialize remains to be seen. The increase in Alberta's recoverable natural gas reserves in 1978 and 1979 were modest, amounting to 1.4 and 1.8 Tcf respectively, and there are good arguments that the NEB projections are overly optimistic.[33] If it turns out they are, natural gas shortages will appear sooner and be larger than illustrated in this figure, and the magnitude of the deficit will swell. Alternatively, larger than currently estimated reserves additions would delay the supply deficits, assuming they were not all exported in the meantime.

Another feature in Chart 3-14 is the relatively minor significance of the known Mackenzie Delta reserves. Those who believe that the frontier areas will provide a panacea for the nation's future energy needs should study this relationship. While the Beaufort Sea reserves potential still remains an unknown despite more than ten years of exploration, even if gas were discovered in significant amounts, the physical, environmental, and social problems that would have to be overcome to make it a practical and reliable source of supply are monumental. For example, problems of containing or controlling shifting ice are truly massive. Thus there is no assurance today that even if sizable reserves exist, the Beaufort Sea can safely be considered a dependable source of future gas supply. The development of technology to contain blowouts or major oil spills in Canadian Arctic waters is in its infancy.[34]

The basic observation here, as in the analysis of the oil supply/demand equation is the fleeting span of time in the existence of this continent during which the accessible hydrocarbon resources in the earth's crust, created over eons of time, will have been dissipated. In the case of natural gas, the way in which exports have helped exhaust Canada's limited supplies prematurely is evident; to a lesser but no less serious extent, exports also have hastened the decline in our reserves of conventional oil. Though it is interesting to speculate what Canadian policy might have been if the true size of the country's recoverable gas and oil reserves had been known in advance – rather than the "hundreds of years supply" promised by the industry – it is not unreasonable to suspect that energy export policy would have been quite different than that followed during the past twenty years. Now that we do know more about Canada's limited recoverable reserves, we can surely hope for a quite different export policy that will conserve our dwindling reserves for Canadians.

But as is apparent from recent NEB and government decisions, it is only a hope. The ability of the producing industry to influence Cana-

CHART 3-14
NATURAL GAS SUPPLY AND DEMAND, CANADA, 1960–2025

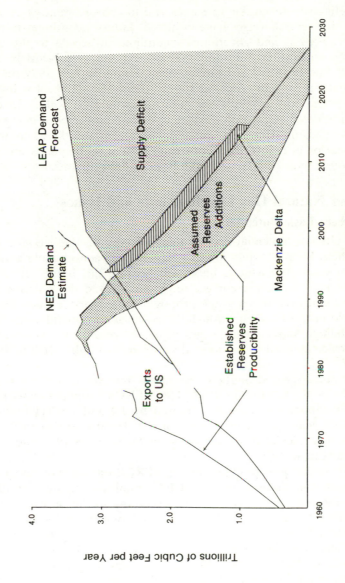

Sources: J.E. Gander and F.W. Belaire, *Energy Futures for Canadians*, Energy, Mines and Resources Canada, Long-term Energy Assessment Program (Ottawa, 1978); National Energy Board, *Gas Report* (Ottawa, 1979).

dian governments and regulatory authorities in the past is clear. They have convinced governments to allow them to export large amounts of depleting non-renewable resources and to approve huge price increases once domestic shortages have occurred. Industry continues to press for export permits and governments continue to accede to the requests. Eleven applications for additional gas exports were heard by the National Energy Board at hearings commencing in July 1979. In view of the natural gas and crude oil supply/demand outlook, it is difficult to understand why a regulatory authority would be willing to consider applications that can only further undermine security of energy supply for Canadians. However, the industry's constant threat to withdraw services or to reduce levels of exploration if its demands are not met obviously must be a factor in the Board's deliberations.

Other Natural Gas Developments and Issues

Southern Basin Potential

The ultimate potential recoverable reserves of the western Canada Southern Basin is a question that has received considerable attention in recent years. The issue is important because this is the supply source for both Canada's present gas requirements and those of the existing export pipelines. It is also the proposed source for the Canadian gas to be sold in U.S. markets through the so-called "pre-build" section of the $23 billion Alaska highway gas pipeline system, the export of which was recommended to the federal government by the NEB in 1979 and 1980.

As noted, proved Southern Basin gas reserves grew only slightly in the 1970s up to January 1978. The AERCB estimates that the provinces's natural gas reserves increased by 1.4 and 1.8 Tcf in 1978 and 1979 respectively, reaching a total of 60.9 Tcf at year-end 1979. The life index was calculated as increasing by 1.0 years in 1978 and declining by 1.6 years in 1979.[35]

The modest growth shown in the AERCB estimates of remaining gas reserves is in sharp contrast to CPA's published figures for 1978 and 1979 for the country as a whole. According to the industry's releases, Canada's "established" – that is, proved plus probable – gas reserves increased by 3.2 Tcf in 1978 and by an astounding 6.1 Tcf in 1979. CPA claims the life index for natural gas leaped ahead from 31.8 years in 1977 to 39.2 years in 1979. The growth in gas reserves occurred mainly in the Arctic Islands and in Alberta.[36]

AERCB reserve estimates are well regarded for their objectivity and are considered to be devoid of any commercial or business interest.

With this in mind, energy planners would be well advised to use the Alberta Board's figures rather than those now put out by CPA. When this is done, the modest growth in Canada's available natural gas reserves throughout the 1970s as shown in Chart 3-10 is supported, and the continuing downward trend in the natural gas life index as illustrated in Chart 3-11 is confirmed. In this way we are better able to understand what appears to be the limited potential for gas reserves growth in the Southern Basin. Such an understanding is important in the face of industry statements and claims which leave a contrary impression.

It is, of course, impossible at this time to predict accurately the magnitude of future gas reserves additions in the Southern Basin or, for that matter, in any of the frontier areas. However, those responsible for Canadian energy policy should keep in mind that

- in spite of the huge wellhead price increases since 1973, annual gas reserve additions have been minimal and the decline in the reserve life index has continued;
- there have been no major gas field discoveries in the Southern Basin for the past ten or more years;
- much of the growth in the 1970s has resulted from the inclusion in recoverable reserves of shallow gas volumes previously known to exist but not considered economic to produce because of small well size and high gathering costs – hence the increase in reserves that has occurred is more a function of changing economics than of successful exploration;
- given that the Southern Basin has been rather intensively explored, it is not logical to expect there will be future major discoveries;
- similarly, lacking new large discoveries, there will be smaller additions because of appreciation, heretofore a principal reason for growth in Canada's recoverable reserves.

This is not to say that the producing industry will cease forecasting immoderate increases in reserves as a consequence of still higher wellhead prices. It is an approach that has been proven financially rewarding to it in the past. Because many billions of dollars are at stake – the selling price of Canada's present oil and gas reserves increases by $18 billion for each $1 hike in the wellhead price of oil – the industry's considerable skills in advancing this argument will be much in evidence. But it should be resisted on the grounds that it has not worked in the past and therefore cannot be expected to work in the future. A much more positive and "fail safe" approach to solving the energy dilemma is required.

Frontier Developments

The situation with respect to the existence of commercially recoverable natural gas reserves in the frontier areas is much the same as with crude oil with the exception of the Mackenzie Delta region, where both this energy policy study and the NEB 1979 *Gas Report* attribute 5.3 Tcf of recoverable reserves to the area. Their future economic availability, while not yet established, is assumed in Chart 3-14.

In its 1979 *Gas Report*, the NEB estimated exploration to date in the Arctic Islands had resulted in 9.2 Tcf of reserves being established, presumably 100 per cent of proved and 50 per cent of probable reserves. The operator in the area, Panarctic Oils Limited, calculated proved, probable, and possible reserves of marketable natural gas of 12.9 Tcf for the same region. Polar Gas Limited, a company established about six years ago to construct and operate an island-hopping pipeline to bring gas from the eastern Arctic south, estimated the same reserves at 11.1 Tcf on a similar basis to that used by Panarctic.[37] It has generally been accepted that a minimum of 20 Tcf of "established" gas reserves are essential before a pipeline would be economically feasible, assuming that it was technologically sound and that it could be safely constructed and operated in a reliable fashion and at an affordable price. In the case of the Polar Gas project this has not yet been tested, although the company maintains that the formidable geographical and environmental barriers can be conquered. In any event, given the slow pace of the development of Arctic Islands reserves, where exploration has been underway for more than ten years, it would appear unwise and certainly premature to count on Arctic Islands gas as an economic future source of energy supply for Canada, even though CPA now includes it in its "established" figure.

Of concern to the prospective viability of the Polar Gas pipeline is the Arctic Pilot Project, a scheme developed by Petro-Canada, the Alberta Gas Trunk Line Company, and Melville Shipping Limited. Involved is the gathering and liquifaction over a twenty-year period of 2 Tcf of Arctic Islands natural gas and its transportation to Atlantic Canada in two 250,000 ton LNG tankers, theoretically capable of breaking their way through ten-foot thick ice. If undertaken, the Arctic Pilot Project would reduce the amount of reserves available to Polar Gas and make its pipeline project that much more difficult to justify and its "threshold" level of reserves more remote. However, it is difficult to see the Arctic Pilot Project as a viable one, given the presently estimated capital cost of $1.6 billion, a figure bound to escalate with time. Also, it is highly conjectural to assume that huge vessels with volatile cargoes can manoeuvre safely and dependably in such a rugged environment. The largest seagoing self-propelled ice-strengthened ship operated by the U.S.S.R. in the High Arctic is only 9,300 tons even though the Soviet Union has, over the past fifty years, built up a significant capability in arctic marine transport.[38] Another aspect affecting the viability of the Arctic Pilot Project is the tie-in it has developed with U.S. pipeline interests that requires the export of 4 Tcf of Southern Basin gas in a complicated arrangement that would further deplete the limited western Canada reserves.

In its 1979 Gas Report, the NEB stated that because of the highly speculative nature of frontier exploration activity, it "did not feel justified in publishing independent forecasts" of reserves additions. Furthermore, the Board pointed out that technological advances for the east coast offshore areas, particularly the Labrador Shelf, undoubtedly would be necessary before commercial production could be anticipated.[39] Therefore, because of an almost complete lack of sufficient information on which to base reserve estimates and the absense of technology even if commercial reserves existed, it is impossible to give any quantitative weight to frontier gas reserves, other than the 5.3 Tcf in the Mackenzie Delta. And because of the extremely high cost of transportation associated with bringing these reserves south, strong reservations as to their likely future availability at affordable costs are in order.

At the same time, it should be pointed out that Dome Petroleum Limited submitted to the NEB hearings its estimates of potential gas reserves for the Beaufort Sea-Mackenzie Delta region of 320 Tcf and for the Arctic Islands 300 Tcf. At this stage, such figures obviously are only guesses. Forecasts of other producing interests were considerably smaller. The Board noted that "the sizable range of estimates of ultimate potential is evidence of the uncertainty that must be attached to the volumes of gas that may be discovered in Canada's frontier areas in the future."[40]

The Pricing of Exported Natural Gas
In 1972 the border price of natural gas exported to the United States was about 40 cents per Mcf (Canadian). By February 1980, the federal government, utilizing a formula that links the export price of Canadian gas to the cost of imported crude oil, had hiked the export price to $4.47 U.S. or about $5.20 Canadian. The early 1980 increase of $1.02 U.S. per Mcf to reach the $4.47 level reflected the OPEC-generated addition of $6.00 U.S. per barrel to the cost of eastern Canadian crude oil imports. Subsequent increases in the cost of foreign oil up to June 1980 normally would call for a further rise in the gas export price of 70 cents U.S. per Mcf. This has not happened as strong U.S. protests over the earlier 1980 hike brought at least a temporary moratorium.

61

Ottawa has agreed to give Washington at least two and a half months notice before imposing still higher prices.

Since the increase to the $4.47 level, two significant developments have occurred. Firstly, the U.S. Federal Energy Regulatory Commission (FERC) indicated that it would begin to limit U.S. imports of Canadian gas to a dollar basis. Thus if Canadian prices went up, volumes would have to decline in order to stay within an overall total dollar amount. Second, present U.S. importers of Canadian gas began to cut back sharply on their purchases. The NEB reports that April 1980 exports were only 56 per cent of the allowable volume compared with 90 per cent a year earlier.[41] Export figures for May indicate the downward trend is continuing, with deliveries amounting to only 56.6 per cent of volumes permitted under existing licenses. Purchases were down everywhere, varying from 38 per cent of that allowed on the Westcoast Transmission system to 72 per cent on the Trans Canada network.[42] It is not unreasonable to conclude that the U.S. government is fed up with the rising price for Canadian gas and is prepared to do something about it. The high cost of Canadian gas supplies is adding to its overall balance of payments deficit even though it may be in surplus with Canada on a bilateral basis. The relatively uniform cutback in U.S. purchases appears to be more than a coincidence and suggests a strategy co-ordinated by the senior government. It is a further indication of the economic power of that country vis-à-vis Canada. While the U.S. appears powerless to do anything about OPEC short of military action, it is able to influence events in Canada and acts accordingly.

The reduction in U.S. gas purchases has the advantage of stretching out the life of Canadian reserves. At the same time it has generated complaints from gas producers and the government of Alberta whose current revenues are being affected. On a national basis Canada's energy costs are increasing because of oil imports and its balance of payments deficit will suffer even more from reduced exports. This is part of the legacy of allowing the eastern third of the country to become and remain dependent on energy imports.

One of the ironies of the situation is that U.S. purchasers are cutting back on their imports of natural gas from Canada at the same time as Canadian producers and pipeline promoters are trying to induce them to take more through the new export "pre-build" scheme. In view of the serious gas supply outlook for Canadians as illustrated by Chart 3-14, it would be a blessing if the "pre-build" project were to collapse and thereby enable Canada to concentrate on solving its energy problems within its own borders. The possibility of such collapse is, in my view, not remote.

The Outlook for Energy Supply from Oil and Gas Combined

Because of today's heavy dependence on oil and natural gas, which together supply nearly 65 per cent of Canada's energy needs, it is instructive to combine the supply/demand projections of the two energy forms in order to examine the outlook for the future for these basic hydrocarbon sources. The following three charts are illustrative. Chart 3-15 shows the rate at which combined proved crude oil, natural gas liquids, and natural gas reserves have increased or decreased in the 1960–78 period. The most striking observation is the great difference between the decades of the 1960s and 1970s. Up to about 1970, significant hydrocarbon reserves additions took place, though the rate declined after peaking in 1964. And, although year-to-year reserves grew in the 1965–69 period, life indices for oil and gas fell because producing rates accelerated faster than reserves. Reserves additions in the 1970s have been highly disappointing. Despite the huge increases in wellhead prices, proved conventional reserves are considerably smaller today than they were ten years ago even when the Mackenzie Delta reserves are included in the totals. Major new oil and gas discoveries have been virtually non-existent in the past ten to fifteen years. Of the additions to reserves since 1970, the Canadian Petroleum Association reports that only 15 per cent came from new finds; the remaining 85 per cent were derived from revisions to previous estimates and extensions to fields previously discovered. Overall it can be expected that CPA will at all times endeavour to maximize its estimates of reserves.

Chart 3-16 plots the manner in which total proved hydrocarbon reserves – including what is referred to as "non-conventional crude oil" namely, the estimated recoverable reserves of synthetic oil from tar sands plants – increased and then decreased during the 1960–78 period. The only two operating tar sands plants are Suncor (formerly Great Canadian Oil Sands) and Syncrude. The former is deemed to have had recoverable reserves of 410 million barrels commencing in 1967; and the latter, reserves of 1,140 million barrels as of 1976. When these reserves additions are added to those of conventional crude oil, the overall result is a slowing of the rate of decline in year-end reserves. The slope of the curve is however, still downward. The addition of Syncrude reserves in 1976 gives the combined oil curve an upward kick but then falls off again for the next two years. It continued its decline in 1979.

When the year-by-year changes in reserves of natural gas liquids are added, both the rate of increase in the 1960s and the rate of decline in the 1970s are accentuated. The addition of the oil equivalent of natural

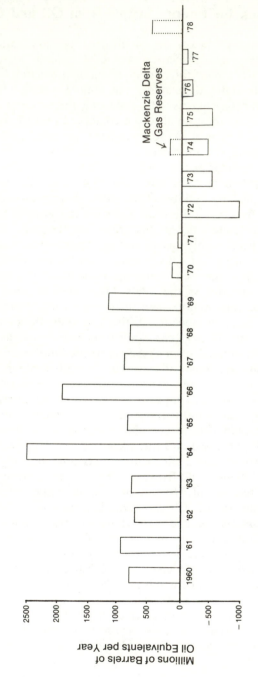

CHART 3-15
PROVED CONVENTIONAL CRUDE OIL, NATURAL GAS LIQUIDS,
AND NATURAL GAS[1] NET ANNUAL RESERVES ADDITIONS, CANADA,
1960–78[2]

[1] Data for natural gas are calculated in barrels of oil equivalents.
[2] Except for 1978 which is probable.

Source: Canadian Petroleum Association *Reserves Committee Report*, 1979.

CHART 3-16
PROVED[1] CONVENTIONAL AND SYNTHETIC OIL AND GAS RESERVES, CANADA, 1950–78

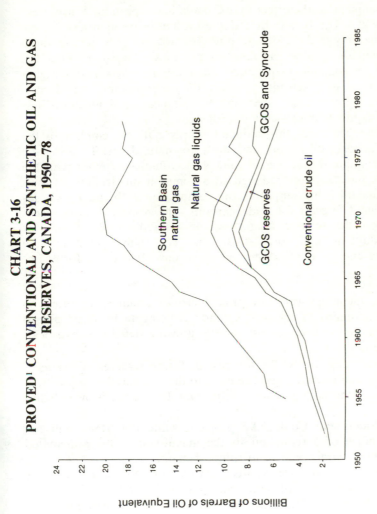

Billions of Barrels of Oil Equivalent

Southern Basin natural gas

Natural gas liquids

GCOS and Syncrude

GCOS reserves

Conventional crude oil

[1] Data are calculated in barrels of oil equivalents from CPA tables of proved year end reserves except for 1978 because of CPA's discontinuance of "proved" category. Changes for 1978 are from CPA's "probable" category, which includes "proved."

Source: Based on data from the Canadian Petroleum Association.

gas reserves (including CPA's 1978 "probable" figure) flattens the rate of overall decline for total hydrocarbons somewhat. But total 1978 year-end reserves amount to only 93 per cent of the 1971 figure.

Many may find this surprising, particularly in light of the strong industry campaign to the effect that Canada has exportable "surpluses" of oil and gas. The fact is that domestic hydrocarbon reserves were down appreciably in the 1970s despite the inclusion of Syncrude and a large amount of shallow gas reserves previously known to exist but considered uneconomic to produce. In addition, when 1970's higher producing rates are taken into account, the life index for all hydrocarbons is much lower today than in 1970, indicating significantly less security of supply than existed a decade ago.

Chart 3-17 bears out this reduced supply outlook, combining the data for Canadian oil supply and those for natural gas. To bring the data to a common basis, the oil and NGL volumes together with the natural gas statistics were reduced to a common quadrillions of Btus (quads) standard. This simplifies the comparison with the LEAP domestic demand forecast for hydrocarbons. The respective areas accurately reflect the relative magnitude of assured supply, hoped-for reserves additions, and forecast deficits. The figures reinforce the problems of energy supply discussed up to now. It is clear, for example, that

- despite the huge wellhead price increases assumed to bring on major additions to reserves, Canada is going to be faced almost immediately with large and rapidly growing deficits in hydrocarbon supply;
- even assuming the NEB's forecast of future reserves additions is correct – and there are good reasons to think it may be optimistic – the size of the supply deficit confronting the country is overwhelming;
- the Alsands and Cold Lake projects, while important, will not make much of a reduction in the magnitude of the anticipated shortfall of supply relative to future demand;
- similarly, the hoped-for results from offshore Newfoundland may not materialize or be of significant magnitude; and
- known Mackenzie Delta gas reserves are minor compared with the estimated future oil and gas requirements of the country.

Thus it is apparent that the rapid build-up in oil and gas producing rates in the 1960s and 1970s took place without much regard for the ability of known reserves to sustain such rates; as a result, anticipated

CHART 3-17
SUPPLY OF AND DEMAND FOR CRUDE OIL, NATURAL GAS LIQUIDS, SYNTHETIC OIL, AND NATURAL GAS, CANADA, 1960–2025

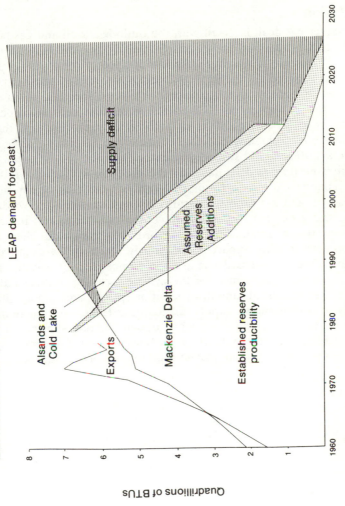

Source: J.E. Gander and F.W. Belaire, *Energy Future for Canadians*, Energy, Mines and Resources Canada Long-term Energy Assessment Program (Ottawa, 1978); National Energy Board, *Oil Report* (Ottawa 1978) and *Gas Report* (Ottawa 1979).

annual production in the 1980s and 1990s will decline rapidly. In my view, the only hope lies in an immediate and massive development of the mineable Athabasca Tar Sands (see Chapter 6).

Conclusion

This chapter has dealt in detail with the outlook for oil and gas because Canada is dependent on these fuels for nearly two-thirds of its energy supply. This is not to minimize the importance of other energy forms, which are examined in the next chapter, but to alert Canadians about the status of their energy resources. Whether adequate oil and gas volumes can be developed to keep the Canadian economy operating for long is a difficult question to answer. The prospects at the moment are indeed gloomy. The trends are all in the wrong direction to achieve a sufficient and sustainable energy supply.

There is no time to delay tackling the problem with all the resources at this country's disposal. From this analysis the lack of foresight in Canada's oil and gas export programs is obvious, while the wisdom of Mexico and a number of the Middle East producing states in limiting current maximum producing rates in order to stretch out their useful lives becomes readily apparent. Obviously, existing Canadian export programs should be phased out as soon as possible. Clearly the policy of relying on the management of the private sector oil and gas industry, which has advocated maximum production, prices, and exports, has led Canada to severe energy supply difficulties. Today's production rates cannot be sustained, and the energy deficit outlook suggests strongly that Canadian industry, regulatory authorities, and governments have not lived up to their duty to protect the interests of Canadians.

The Outlook For Other Energy Supplies

4

Because of the apparent limited magnitude of accessible conventional oil and gas reserves, it is important that all other possible energy sources be investigated and analysed even though industry data may be sketchy at this time. This chapter examines the outlook for uranium, coal, and renewable supplies including hydro-electricity.

Uranium

Many who have been concerned with the finite nature and rate of depletion of North America's oil and gas reserves have been comforted by the impression that the world contained nearly boundless reserves of fissionable uranium that could be harnessed to provide virtually unlimited energy supplies for the future. Proponents of nuclear power have pointed out that even if the quantities of fissile uranium 233 and 235 turn out to be limited, the breeder reactor that produces more fissile nuclei than it destroys can be developed to meet man's continuing energy needs. While recognizing the ongoing debate over nuclear power and the controversial nature of the issues, this section does not consider the technological and security concerns related to the breeder reactor, the complex health and safety aspects of nuclear power, or the problems associated with handling and storage of radioactive wastes.[1] Rather, this section looks briefly only at the issue of uranium supply and demand both worldwide and in Canada, and compares forecasts of future requirements with known and inferred quantities of reserves.

Worldwide Outlook

The World Energy Conference (WEC) recently studied future global energy demand and the likely availability of various forms of energy supply.[2] In its assessment the WEC predicted that world energy demand will increase from 310 quads in 1980 to 1,000 quads in 2020, even though the average growth in demand in OECD countries will be limited to 1.1 per cent per year. With respect to electricity, the WEC forecast that total demand will grow by 750 per cent from 20.5 to 173 exajoules between 1972 and 2020, a rate of increase that is 50 per cent faster than that of total primary energy. This growth reflects, in large part, the assumption that electricity will be called upon to fill the increasing gap between total energy demand and the supply of oil, gas, coal, and renewables. This huge growth in demand for electricity, coupled with limited availability of new hydro-electric sites, implies a requirement for 5 million megawatts of nuclear electric generating capacity by the year 2020, compared with 76,000 megawatts in existence in 1975. By 2020, therefore, nuclear plants are assumed to be supplying 60 to 65 per cent of total electricity requirements. In order to stretch out uranium supplies, the WEC predicted that breeder reactors would be introduced in the late 1980s. With breeder reactors, cumulative global demand for uranium would reach 9.5 million tonnes by 2020. Without breeders cumulative demand would be 13.9 million tonnes.

World known uranium production capability is forecast to increase from 33,000 tonnes per year in 1977 to 109,000 tonnes by 1990 and then decline to half that level by 2020. Even with the development of breeder reactors, a course of action so far rejected both by U.S. President Carter and by Ontario's Royal Commission on Electric Power Planning, uranium production based on today's known reserves would be capable of meeting only 13 per cent of forecast demand in the year 2020.

Chart 4-1 illustrates the WEC projection of the uranium supply/demand outlook. The supply gap commencing in 1990 is huge, growing rapidly with time. To close it by 2020 would require the discovery of 330 new average-size uranium mines by 2015.[3] One has to question seriously whether it is reasonable to assume that such a discovery rate is possible, let alone likely.

Canadian Outlook

In the face of an anticipated much reduced role for crude oil in meeting Canada's overall energy requirements, the LEAP report called for a greatly expanded role for nuclear generated electricity. To increase its forecast contribution to total energy supply from 2 to 18 per cent as needed (see Table 2-2), nuclear power would have to expand by 1600 per cent by the year 2000 and by 2400 per cent by 2025 over Canada's nuclear capacity in 1975. Such a program would require enormous increases in the domestic uranium supply, as well as a construction program of unprecedented proportions.

Chart 4-2 illustrates the amount of uranium that would be required to fuel the reactors called for in the LEAP program. Annual require-

70

CHART 4-1
URANIUM SUPPLY/DEMAND, OECD COUNTRIES, 1975–2025

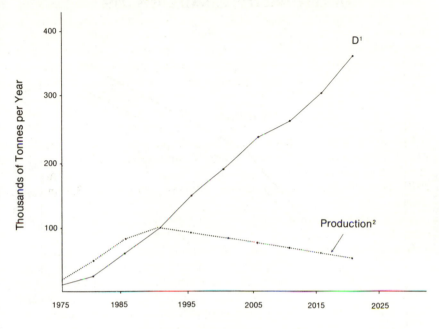

[1] Assumes breeder reactors are introduced in the 1980s.

[2] From known sources.

Source: Paper presented by Gordon McNabb, president, Uranium Canada Limited, at *Financial Post* conference, Vancouver 1979.

ments would increase from 200 tonnes in 1975 to 3,800 tonnes in 2000 and to 5,500 tonnes in 2025. Installed operating nuclear generating capacity, which was approximately 3,000 megawatts in 1975, would total 67,000 megawatts by the year 2000 and 99,000 megawatts by 2025.

While it might be argued that the LEAP program is far too ambitious and that the amounts of uranium it theoretically would require greatly overstate what Canada's actual needs will be, it is well to keep in mind that LEAP's requirements for oil and gas are anything but assured, that mammoth hydrocarbon supply deficits are likely to occur, and that as a result Canada's real need for electric energy as a replacement for fossil fuels could turn out to be much larger than postulated in the LEAP report. In any event, the current rate of construction of new nuclear generating capacity falls far short of the pace required to achieve the LEAP projection of meeting 15 per cent of Canada's total energy needs with nuclear power by 2000.

CHART 4-2
ANNUAL URANIUM REQUIREMENTS FOR PRODUCTION
OF ELECTRICITY, CANADA, 1975–2025

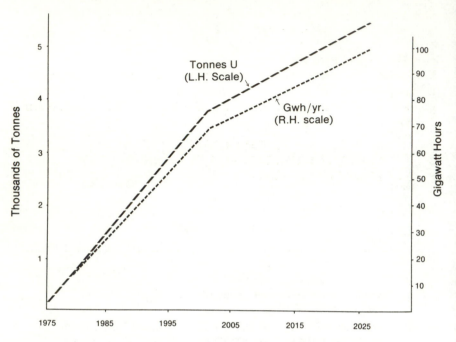

Source: Based on data from J.E. Gander and F.W. Belaire, *Energy Futures for Canadians* (LEAP) (Ottawa: Energy, Mines and Resources Canada, 1978).

Chart 4-3 shows Ontario Hydro's April 1979 nuclear power construction program until 1990.[4] Superimposed on the Ontario program are the rated capacities of Canada's only other nuclear installations, Quebec's Gentilly and New Brunswick's Point Lepreau generating stations. It should be noted, however, that Gentilly 1 was closed indefinitely in July 1979 because of continuing technical problems, having produced virtually no commercial power in seven of the past eight years and that Gentilly 2 and Point Lepreau are still under construction.[5] In addition, because of a recent slowing in the growth in demand for electric power, Ontario Hydro has decided to proceed with its Bruce B and Darlington nuclear stations on a slower schedule than originally contemplated. If this revised plan is followed, it appears that Canada will have about 15,000 megawatts of nuclear generating capacity by 1992, only about one-third of which would be required to achieve the level of capacity required by the LEAP allocation of total energy demand. With this much-reduced availability of electric energy, it clearly is not realistic to expect the large substitution of electric for oil-based energy to take place as envisaged in the LEAP report, at least in the period to the end of the century.

Uranium Export Policy
Ever since the early 1940s, Canada has been exporting substantial amounts of uranium to the United States, primarily for that country's military weapons program. Since the late 1960s, Canadian uranium

CHART 4-3
CURRENT PROGRAM FOR DEVELOPMENT OF
NUCLEAR GENERATING CAPACITY, CANADA, 1975–2025

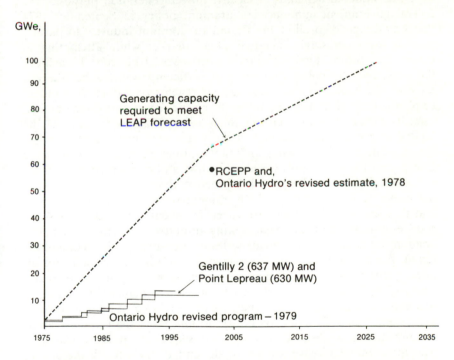

Source: Based on data from J.E. Gander and F.W. Belaire, *Energy Futures for Canadians* (LEAP) (Ottawa: Energy, Mines and Resources Canada, 1978); Ontario Hydro; and Ontario Royal Commission on Electric Power Planning.

73

also has helped satisfy the growing international demand for civilian nuclear power developments. Because of the still modest annual uranium requirements associated with Canada's own nuclear power program, the uranium mining industry in this country has been developed around an export, rather than a domestic, market. Productive mining and milling capacity is currently being expanded primarily for export markets. According to data contained in the Interim Report of Ontario's Royal Commission on Electric Power Planning (Porter Commission), existing export commitments of 73,400 tonnes amount to 40 per cent of Canada's presently known uranium reserves in the measured and indicated categories.[6] If the "inferred" reserve category is included in the assumed supply base, existing export commitments drop to less than 20 per cent of total uranium reserves. However, opinions vary about the degree of reliability that should be attached to the inferred category.[7]

Because of the strategic importance of uranium and the potentiall[y] huge international demand for electric power generation purposes, the federal government announced a uranium policy in September 1974 that was designed to allow the Canadian uranium industry to participate in the increasingly lucrative world market while attempting to ensure that future domestic market needs would be met. To achieve this objective, the policy requires that sufficient uranium be reserved for domestic use to enable each nuclear reactor operating, committed, or planned ten years into the future to be fuelled at an average annual capacity factor of 80 per cent for thirty years; that export contracts be limited to a maximum duration of ten years, with contingent approval for an additional five years; and that utilities maintain a contracted fifteen-year forward supply for all operating and committed reactors.[8]

Statistical data on the growth of recoverable uranium reserves are not available from industry or government sources to the same extent that they are for oil and gas. However, in recent years, Energy, Mines and Resources Canada has been making annual assessments of Canada's uranium reserves in all three categories of measured, indicated, and inferred. According to its 1977 assessment, total adjusted reserves for all three categories grew by less than 4 per cent between year-end 1976 and year-end 1977.[9] This is a small increase when it is realized that exploration expenditures for uranium increased from $43.5 million in 1976 to $71.7 million in 1977 and exploratory drilling more than doubled from 137,300 metres to 293,400 metres.[10] Consequently, it is questionable whether uranium discoveries can be depended upon to fill the gap in Canadian uranium requirements to the end of the century or beyond, as forecast in LEAP.

Between 1973 and 1977 the world price of uranium rose dramatically from $17 to $110 per kilo, an increase of 550 per cent. This immense price hike resulted from actions taken by a producer's cartel of which Canada, apparently, was one of the participants. While this high price together with an export-oriented producing industry may be helpful in the short run in reducing Canada's international balance-of-payments deficit, in the longer run future uranium supplies for Canadian reactors will be reduced and costs for Canadian consumers increased.

In its interim report, the Porter Commission tested the formula against two Ontario Hydro forward estimates of Canadian nuclear power capacity in the year 2000.[11] These were 82,000 megawatts, Hydro's initial estimate for the country as a whole in that year, and 60,000 megawatts, Hydro's revised forecast. (see Chart 4-3) The latter figure is close to the 67,000 megawatt estimate in this study developed from the LEAP projection. The Porter Commission included the "inferred" category of reserves in its assumed supply base but discounted it by 30 per cent to reflect the unreliability of the estimate. It also discounted the "indicated" category by 20 per cent for the same reason. When these amounts were added to the "measured" category, the Commission arrived at a total current "adjusted reserve" for Canada as a whole of 377,000 tonnes, 282,000 of which were in Ontario.

Using the federal formula to calculate uranium requirements and forward commitments up to the year 2000, the Commission found that the 82,000 megawatts domestic program plus existing export commitments would require a total of 513,000 tonnes of uranium if the policy standards were to be met, and the 60,000 megawatts program would require 407,000 tonnes. Since both estimates of potential requirements exceeded the adjusted reserve including the "inferred" category – the 82,000 megawatts case by 36 per cent, the 60,000 megawatts case by 8 per cent – the Porter Commission was concerned that the policy formula, while appearing to guarantee that domestic requirements would be met, indicates that presently known reserves would not be adequate for either of the two cases examined for the year 2000. On the basis of these two projections, therefore, it could be argued that Canada is already overcommitted to uranium exports if domestic needs are to be fully protected up to 2000 – which is less than twenty years away – let alone beyond that point.

The Porter Commission was also concerned about two additional points. First, despite the very large and lucrative uranium contract entered into by Ontario Hydro with producers in 1978, priority given to existing export contracts by those producers will result in some shortfalls in uranium supply for Hydro until 1993. The shortfalls will be met either from production outside Ontario or by dipping into federal stockpiles. Second, the timing of production for export will likely lead mining companies to export the higher grade more profitable reserves and then argue that later production for domestic markets should command higher prices because of increased costs.

The similarity of the methods used by both the uranium and petroleum industries is striking, and in both industries past practice has benefitted producers at the expense of consumers. Canada's role as supplier of energy resources to the rest of the world as practised by industry – while alleging future domestic needs are being protected – will have huge long-term costs for the Canadian economy.

Coal

The Workshop on Alternative Energy Strategies recently concluded in its report, *Energy: Global Prospects*, that at the world's current rate of coal consumption economically recoverable reserves would last over 200 years. The WAES report put world measured reserves of coal at 1,327 billion tonnes and economically recoverable reserves at 737 billion tonnes.[12] Over 70 per cent of these reserves are located in the U.S.S.R., China, and the United States, with the United States alone accounting for over 30 per cent of world supplies. The WAES report went on to stress lack of reliability of coal reserve estimates and to state that international coal reserves are likely to be greater than those figures imply: "The picture for coal is less clear than for oil because exploration has been less widespread and generally less intensive. Many estimates of coal reserves were made during an era when readily available, low-cost oil was rapidly displacing coal, resulting in little incentive to look for coal."[13] Consequently, for the next century at least, there is little doubt that on a worldwide basis reserves would be adequate to support increased use of that energy resource. However, a number of other factors constitute major constraints to its being used in additional ways.

The first concern is environmental. Can coal utilization be increased without placing unacceptable strains on the environment through sulphur dioxide, sulphate, and nitrate emissions? Acid rain and increased human morbidity rates have been directly attributed to such emissions. In addition, there are serious concerns that large increases in the use of coal will raise the carbon dioxide levels in the atmosphere to the point where a "greenhouse effect" will cause a rise in the surface temperature of the earth. The ensuing climatological shifts would have enormous consequences. Also, large-scale coal mining and transportation operations can have major detrimental effects on specific areas. For example, strip-mining practices have left large scars on the landscape in certain regions, although modern practice has been to insist on surface reclamation.

The second constraint relates to the fact that the energy end-uses to which coal can be directly put are severely limited. A major role for coal would be to replace oil and gas. However, coal gasification and liquefaction would be required to make the fuel useful for many applications, and current technology is expensive and in many instances underdeveloped. Nevertheless, as prices rise, synthetic fuels become increasingly competitive.

Finally, there is the interrelated question of the effort and financial expenditure required to increase the production and transportation of coal. Enormous investments, long lead times, and great amounts of international and interregional planning and co-ordination would be required to get the coal out of the ground and to the locations where it could be used.

Canadian Supply Outlook

Coal previously played a much greater role in the nation's energy supply than it does today, providing close to half of Canada's energy requirements as recently as 1950. But with ever-increasing quantities of oil and gas at progressively lower real costs, coal consumption declined steadily during the 1950s and 1960s. House heating, rail transportation, and industrial processes among others shifted from coal use to other fuels. As a result, the coal industry suffered a large decline, especially in eastern Canada, though during the 1970s, the industry underwent a slight resurgence mainly because of increased exports of metallurgical coal.

Today coal is frequently identified as an alternative energy source to which the industrialized nations can turn to substitute for declining oil and gas supplies. President Carter has made increased coal use a key component of his energy strategy, for example, and it has been suggested that the Canadian government will place a similar priority on coal. The LEAP report argues that a more than threefold increase in coal use to 1990 with a further doubling to 2025 will be necessary.

To what extent can Canadian coal resources support increased requirements? What problems would significantly increased consumption of Canadian coal present? In 1977 Canada consumed about 34 million tons of coal, which represented about 8 per cent of the nation's primary energy supply and produced about 31 million tons. To some observers, this suggests that Canada is close to self-sufficiency in coal, with net imports of only about 3 million tons. However, this is somewhat misleading in that about half of Canadian consumption, or 17 million tons, was imported – a result of the large distances between Ontario and the west, the main Canadian consumers and producers of coal respectively, and of the availability to Ontario of large quantities of comparatively economic U.S. coal. Indeed, U.S. measured reserves are over thirty times greater than Canada's, and its economically recoverable reserves are about forty times greater. This underlines one of the problems that will have to be overcome if Canada is to increase its use of domestically produced coal.

Primarily because of the decline of coal use and the lack of strategic priority placed on coal, comparatively little is known about the extent of Canada's coal resources. Recognizing this large data gap, the federal government moved in the mid-1970s to establish a national coal inventory program. Provincial governments took action as well and British Columbia, Alberta, and Saskatchewan have stepped up efforts to delineate their coal resources. The present state of knowledge is, however, slender. Consequently, the following estimates must be regarded with caution.

The most recent data available on a nation-wide basis are contained in the federal government document, *Coal Resources and Reserves of Canada,* published December in 1979.[14] The report contains estimates of both coal resources and reserves. The report estimates the quantity of Canada's coal resources under three different categories – measured, inferred, and indicated – for a number of different types of coal. Table 4-1, which summarizes these estimates, suggests that Canada has enormous coal resources. At the level of current consumption, the measured resources would last more than 1400 years; even at a rate of annual consumption five times the present 35 million tons, the resources would last close to three centuries. However, these data do not adequately gauge the coal available for consumption. As defined in the report, coal *reserves* refer to "a portion of the measured and indicated resources with due regard to current technology and economics"[15]; and it is the reserves category that is of greatest interest for purposes of evaluating coal resources potentially available for utilization. The EMR report goes on to describe a further category of reserves termed "recoverable" coal, or the portion of mineable coal that can be recovered with current technology at current market prices in areas where coal mining is legally permitted. The quantity of recoverable coal is estimated at 5,906 million tons. Though this figure is tentative and may prove conservative, it is useful to consider what level of consumption this quantity of reserves would support.

The LEAP report recommended an increase in coal utilization from the current 34 million tons to 112 million tons by 1990, 120 million tons

TABLE 4-1
ESTIMATED QUANTITY OF COAL RESOURCES, CANADA,
BY PROVINCE, 1978
(millions of short tons in place)

	Resources of Immediate and Future Interest		
	Measured	Indicated	Inferred
Nova Scotia	226	593	885
New Brunswick	32	16	1
Ontario	218	—	—
Saskatchewan	1,660	6,594	26,948
Alberta	39,300	—	326,700
British Columbia	9,127	9,989	51,475
Canada	50,563	17,192	406,009

Source: Energy, Mines and Resources, *Coal Resources and Reserves of Canada*, ER 79-9 (Ottawa, 1979).

by 2000, and 200 million tons by 2025.[17] Chart 4-4 shows what would happen to the approximately 6,000 million tons of recoverable reserves if they were depleted at this rate. The chart demonstrates that no reserves would remain in 2025; all of the recoverable coal would be depleted.

Some critics have argued that the "recoverable coal" category is not relevant for purposes of assessing the amount of coal available for future use and have suggested that mineable coal provides a better gauge. Mineable coal reserves are estimated to be in the order of 16,000 million tons, a little over 2.7 times the recoverable reserves. Assuming no increase in the LEAP estimated consumption for 2025 of 200 million tons per year, mineable coal reserves would last approximately fifty years beyond 2025.

This does not mean that Canada cannot turn to coal for a greater proportion of its energy needs, especially over the next thirty to fifty years, which is the critical period during which the bulk of the world's petroleum resources will be exhausted. However, it does suggest that indigenous coal does not provide a sustainable substitute for petroleum as Canada's major energy source. It also suggests that further clarification of the extent of Canada's economically accessible coal reserves is required before any move is made to a major and long-term increased commitment to domestic coal utilization for either conventional or synthetic oil and gas purposes.

CHART 4-4
COAL CONSUMPTION AND REMAINING COAL RESERVES, CANADA, 1975–2025

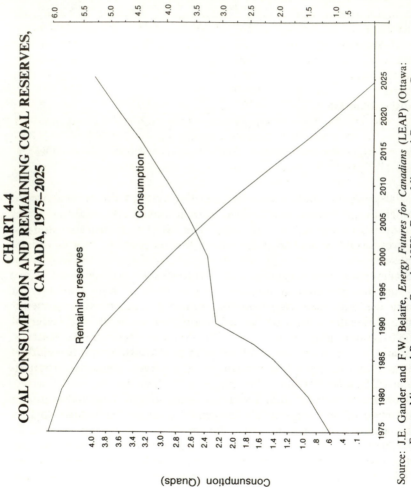

Source: J.E. Gander and F.W. Belaire, *Energy Futures for Canadians* (LEAP) (Ottawa: Energy, Mines and Resources Canada, 1978); Energy Mines and Resources Canada, *Coal Resources and Reserves* of Canada, ER 79-9 (Ottawa, 1979).

Renewable Energy Resources

Renewable energy resources, broadly defined, include all energy sources that directly utilize the earth's energy income – primarily solar energy – rather than the depletable energy capital accumulated in the form of fossil fuels or fissile materials such as uranium. The primary forms of these sources are hydro-electricity derived from falling water, direct solar energy, biomass energy from conversion of plant and animal material, and wind energy. Other sources sometimes classified as renewables are tidal power and geothermal energy.[18] Renewables offer one of the few alternate resources upon which a sustainable energy future can be based.[19] Thus they are strategic to long-term energy supply.

Hydro-electricity

Hydraulic energy, created by storing water at higher elevations and releasing it at controlled rates through turbines and waterwheels to drive electricity-producing generators, has been employed by man for decades to produce increasing amounts of electric energy. This process is really a highly sophisticated way of converting solar energy – sunshine, air currents, moisture-carrying capacity, and the earth's topography – into an efficient and flexible form of renewable energy supply. This type of energy has been developed in impressive projects throughout the world, and Canadian engineers, whose expertise has increased with successively large and complex domestic projects, have played important roles in recent years in the design and construction of hydro installations in third world countries.

Unfortunately, there are physical and economic limits to the amounts of hydraulic energy that can be generated to meet rising world energy demand and to offset declining supplies of non-renewable fossil fuels. The size of the rivers, the generosity of nature in providing suitable dam sites and their location relative to load centres, the environmental losses suffered by flooding agricultural lands, and the need to preserve many streams for the fish cycle all work to put a ceiling on the quantities of hydraulic energy that can be counted upon to supply industrialized economies.

According to the World Energy Conference report, hydro-electric energy supplied about 6 per cent of total world energy production in 1972.[20] In comparison, oil provided 47 per cent, coal 27 per cent, and natural gas 19 per cent of the total, while nuclear electricity contributed less than 1 per cent. After a careful review of worldwide hydraulic resource potential, the report forecast that by 2020 hydro-electric power may have increased its share of the much larger total energy requirement to 6.5 per cent. Nevertheless, even if that growth is achievable, hydraulic energy will do very little to replace dwindling supplies of nonrenewable resources.

Hydro-electric power has long been the backbone of Canada's electricity generating systems. In 1975 it constituted 63 per cent of total installed capacity and over 70 per cent of net electrical generation.[21] The magnitude of Canada's hydro power and the manner of its development are impressive by world standards. On the basis of the LEAP report tabulation, hydraulic energy is expected to increase its output to 2.52 quads by the year 2000 and to 2.63 quads by 2025 from 1.74 quads in 1975. However, given the nation's continually growing overall energy requirement, hydro-electric's share of the total is projected to drop from 22 per cent of primary energy demand in 1975 to 16 per cent by 2000 and to 13 per cent by 2025.

This declining share results from the fact that most of the larger, accessible hydro sites have already been utilized. As the sites closer to the urban centres became developed (Niagara and Ottawa Rivers, the St. Lawrence Seaway, Manicouagan, and the St. John and Bow Rivers), new hydro projects have been undertaken further afield at Churchill Falls in Labrador, the Peace River in British Columbia, the Nelson River in Manitoba, and James Bay in Quebec. Additional hydro potential is located in James Bay, Gull Island, Labrador, the Nelson and Churchill Rivers in Manitoba, and the Peace River in Alberta and British Columbia. There are also a few sites in the Yukon and Northwest Territories, although distances from present load centres make them less attractive.

By the year 2000 very few, if any, developable sites are likely to remain. The LEAP demand estimates project a 45 per cent increase in hydro-electric generation between 1975 and 2000, but only a 5 per cent rise from the 2000 to 2025 period. This reflects the anticipated mature state of hydro-electric developments in Canada by the end of this century. New forms of hydraulic energy may be developed – tidal, wave, low hydraulic head, pumped storage from wind power – but they will all be relatively high cost and of limited magnitude. Also, environmental and ecological constraints will act to help limit maximum theoretical hydro developments from coast to coast. Thus the LEAP projection of the future availability of hydro-electric energy appears reasonable and is not likely to be exceeded.

Other Renewable Energy Resources

Direct solar, biomass, and wind energy do not currently contribute a large share to Canada's national energy supply. Wood is an important energy resource in some of the less urbanized parts of the country where approximately 140,000 homes are presently heated by this energy form.[22] Wood is also an important energy resource for the pulp and paper industry, where wood waste is used extensively as "hog fuel". Wind power, once a major source of energy on the nation's farms, is beginning to reappear in demonstration programs of windmill generated electricity. While there are a number of potential applications for wind energy, the most relevant appears to be windmill-generated electricity for offgrid and even grid use. The number of direct solar applications is small but growing.

Direct solar applications fall naturally into two categories: solar thermal and solar electric. Solar thermal applications include space and water heating for use in the residential, commercial, and industrial sectors as well as process heating for industrial purposes. In the case of solar space heating, both active and passive techniques can be employed. Active solar techniques employ solar heating systems – including solar collectors, thermal storage, and circulation systems – to capture and distribute heat from the sun. Rather than using systems with moving parts, passive techniques draw on measures such as building design and orientation and choice of materials for building construction to utilize the heat from the sun more fully. For example, increasing the window area on the south side of a building is a passive solar technique. Both of these approaches are currently in use; passive techniques have shown themselves economic in a wide range of applications. While active solar space and water heating systems require significant capital outlay, they already have proven economic in some parts of the country.

Photovoltaic cells transform solar energy directly into electric current. This proven technology, which emerged from the space program and is presently restricted to applications such as remote signalling and sensing devices where its current high cost is not a barrier, is potentially the most important solar electric technology for Canada. It has been suggested that with improvements in production processes and much longer production runs, both of which are considered possible in the next decade, a major cost reduction in photovoltaics would occur and open a mass market for the technology, enabling it to provide a significant share of the industrialized world's electrical requirements in the future.[23]

Biomass energy is available from a variety of different plant and animal sources: forest waste, currently undercut or underutilized wood, tree plantations, other crops, animal waste, and urban solid waste. Direct thermal applications for biomass include the burning of wood for residential space heating. Electricity can also be generated using wood directly, as in the case of the installation at Summerside, Prince Edward Island, or by burning wood that has already been gasified.

Biomass, very importantly, can also be converted into liquid forms for use as a substitute for petroleum products, primarily in the transportation sector. Ethanol or methanol can be produced from a range of sources using a variety of different methods. The "gasohol" that has been used in the United States, for example, is ethanol distilled from grain. Present day gasohol is a mixture of 90 per cent gasoline and 10 per cent ethanol. Large-scale production of methanol from wood, using a two-step gasification and liquefaction process, is feasible but expensive.

Renewables and Energy Policy

Renewable energy sources share a number of significant advantages. They tend to be relatively clean and safe and appear to have few negative environmental consequences. Some of the technologies are well developed, others less so. Many applications such as solar space and water heating are end-use specific and employed at the point where the energy is captured; for example, the house being heated. Much of the economic activity associated with the manufacturing and installation of the technologies is similarily decentralized. These sources tend to be more amenable to decentralized development and do not require large geographic concentrations of capital and labour as do projects such as the tar sands and pipelines, for example. Thus they appeal to the "small is beautiful" advocates.

The question today is what contribution renewable energy can make to energy supply. There are many reasons the answer to this question is relatively uncertain at this point. The first relates to the "newness" of the technology, which may not be either fully developed or whose economic benefits are uncertain, or some of both. This is true for photovoltaics for example. It is also true that while the technology may be developed, as in the case of solar space heating, a mass market does not currently exist. Consequently it is difficult to be confident about the large-scale adoption of a technology. In addition the kind of analysis of end-use implementation and penetration that is required to assess the potential of renewable energy is itself new and there is inadequate experience with these techniques to be really confident in the results they produce.

A number of different estimates of renewable energy potential have been made. The LEAP report does not attempt to disaggregate potential by type of renewable energy source, but it forecasts that renewables will be developed to a level where they will be supplying 0.8 quads in 2000 or 5 per cent of total primary energy demand and 2.0 quads or 10 per cent by 2025.[24] The Science Council of Canada estimated that by 2025 solar thermal could contribute 2.2 quads of energy; biomass, 1.8

84

quads; solar electric, 0.4 quads; and wind power, 0.05 quads.[25] This gives a total of 4.45 quads, about double the LEAP estimate. Amory Lovins concluded that solar thermal and biomass resources could yield about 5.0 quads by 2025 without including solar electric or wind potential in his estimate.[26] Lovins' figures are 25 per cent higher than those of the Science Council. A study done by the Workgroup on Energy Policy suggested a potential of about 12 quads by the year 2025 for renewables.[27]

In part these variations in assessments are attributable to disagreements about what is technically and economically possible. Most of the variation, however, is due to the intensity with which it is assumed the implementation of the renewables is pursued. Estimating potential for renewables presents the same sort of problem as estimating potential for energy conservation. A wide range appears to be possible; within limits, the potential depends on what we want that potential to be. This is not as true in the short to medium term, where physical and other constraints of moving to a large renewable component are significant, as it is for the longer range. It appears we can choose to have a relatively low or relatively high contribution from renewables in the longer term.

Most analysts agree, however, that there are important barriers that must be overcome if renewables are to make a signficant, let alone major, contribution. For example, infrastructure for production, marketing, and distribution of solar energy must be developed; issues, such as "right to light" bylaws that place restrictions on solar use, must be resolved; high initial costs of many renewable applications must be reduced; consumers must be made aware of and accept the technology; and, of course, technical innovation must proceed apace.

Still renewables have a unique and vital role to play. They embody the foundations of a sustainable energy future. Their ability to solve our problems to the turn of the century is limited, but in the longer term they have significant potential. If efforts are not made now to encourage that long-range potential it may never materialize or will develop too late. We will, of necessity rather than choice, be locked into a future dominated by scarcity and its accompanying severe economic consequences or by reliance on advanced nuclear fission cycles with their inherent hazards and uncertainties. The role of renewables must be an integral part of a full assessment of how to achieve a sustainable long-range energy future.

Regardless of what is decided about the ultimate role for renewables and the precise timing of their entry, governments must be committed to overcoming the obstacles that currently lie in the path of their development. While a premium should be placed on renewables because of their special characteristics, we cannot rely on the market to develop them so they will be ready when needed. A range of government measures from incentives through to education programs and, perhaps, direct government action must be established. The federal government has taken the first tentative steps in this direction with increases in research and development spending for renewables. The United States has gone much further, both at the federal and state levels, with incentives for solar heating, elimination of some problematic bylaws, and encouragement for gasohol production and use.

Conclusion

Given the high degree of dependency on energy Canadians have developed, the finite nature of the depleting supplies from non-renewable sources on which we now rely, and the inability to date of governments and industry to evolve new commercial supplies from advanced technology, it is apparent that future generations will have to obtain most if not all their essential energy requirements from renewable sources if comfortable lifestyles are to be sustained. One of the great present imponderables is the type of society and level of living standards that such renewable sources will support. But the longer the delay in tackling the energy issues with vision and vigour, the worse off Canadians will be. For example, today's food production is only possible because of the energy subsidy agriculture receives. If the world runs out of fossil and nuclear fuels, food producers will have to revert to "primitive" systems based on solar energy – which would clearly be a step backward for mankind.

Canada's Energy Problems: The Legacy of the Past

5

In the past ten to fifteen years, the industrialized world's heavy and sometimes profligate use of energy resources predictably has caught up with finite supply. As is evident from the analysis in Chapters 3 and 4, Canada faces large shortages of oil and gas within a very few years and other energy forms are not unlimited. Even though this country is believed to be among the best endowed in the industrialized world in terms of resources, the declining magnitude of established oil and gas reserves, the finite nature of mineable coal and uranium, and the limited number of undeveloped hydro-electric sites all lead inescapably to the certainty that, given our current course, and barring economic collapse that might result from the effect of rapidly escalating prices or other factors, overall energy demand will significantly outstrip domestic supply within the foreseeable future. This would be true even if energy demand growth rates were cut in half during the next two decades and more than halved again after 2000.

Nor should Canada look to imports to solve the physical supply problem. World reserves of crude oil, the most important and easily deliverable energy form, will soon decline if they have not already started to do so. Most reserves are in the control of a politically unstable cartel and, in any case, this nation cannot afford to worsen its already serious balance-of-payments problems by bringing in still larger shipments of excessively priced crude oil.

Understandably, some may be confused about the adequacy of future domestic oil and gas supplies. The media frequently report that new developments, such as recent discoveries or prospective reductions in demand, have eliminated the spectre of shortages, for unstated periods. Such claims may, of course, be true if the period examined is short enough or the region in question small enough. At the same time, however, it should be remembered that the validity of such information and the reasons for its release must be assessed carefully, as stock market manipulation based on incomplete or misleading data is not an unknown phenomena in the financial markets of North America. This report was designed to concentrate on long-term trends and analyses, for only when the longer term is examined does the serious nature of the difficulties facing Canada emerge.

As was clearly demonstrated in Chart 3-7 the producibility of Canada's domestic crude oil sources is dropping rapidly. This trend will continue until presently known fields are virtually exhausted by about 2000. The addition of synthetic oil production from the Suncor and Syncrude plants plus hoped-for future discoveries of conventional crude do little to change the basic shape of the anticipated oil availability curves. If the Alsands and Cold Lake projects go forward, despite the threats of their sponsors to withhold their services unless further tax and other concessions are granted, some reduction in the magnitude of the future supply deficit will occur. But the additional production from these projects will still leave total supply far short of meeting even the reduced demand levels forecast in the LEAP study.[1] Possible frontier sources are too nebulous and uncertain to be counted on at this time.

The natural gas supply outlook, while marginally better than that for crude oil, provides no reason for complacency. As shown in Chart 3-14, production from known reserves plus assumed additions is forecast to decline within ten years. Within twenty years, total gas production including that from the Mackenzie Delta will be substantially lower than estimated Canadian requirements. A rapidly increasing supply deficit of ominous proportions is approaching for the twenty-first century. The deficit will occur before 1990 if the perhaps too generous assumptions of the National Energy Board about future production fail to materialize. Alternatively, if ultimate reserves prove to be larger than forecast and are developed in a timely way, the "cross-over point," when supply becomes inadequate, might occur somewhat later.

The possibility of the shortfall occurring later rather than sooner is unlikely. The natural gas industry, including Canadian distribution companies with producing interests, appears dedicated to rapid use of reserves as soon as they are discovered. The industry's philosophy that seeks to export reserves in excess of immediate Canadian needs is not geared to the long-term protection of Canadian requirements. Indeed, the National Energy Board in its 1979 gas export hearings faced a large group of production, transmission, and distribution companies who unanimously advocated stepped-up exports to the United States, despite the Board's own report of February 1979 that foresaw growing Canadian supply deficiencies as soon as 1984 on the basis of presently known reserves and by 1992 assuming major future reserves additions. Industry argues that increased exports will accelerate exploration and generate new supplies. This is a curious theory when applied to a finite non-renewable resource, but it has been accepted by Canadian authorities.

In the past, the Board has found the arguments of the producer interests for maximum production and higher profits convincing and has recommended greater exports, despite its own longer range projections. Therefore, it is unlikely that Canadian consumers, who have largely financed whatever increase in reserves has resulted from exploration paid for by the massive price increases of the past six years, will benefit from an enhanced supply base. If industry has its way, additional reserves will have been exported by the time domestic markets have grown to the point where they can be utilized in Canada. It is indeed ironic – and a measure of the influence of the oil industry with the federal government – that the much higher prices now being paid by Canadians for domestic production have funded the exploration that is the basis for the new wave of export applications.

The combined oil and gas supply/demand outlook in Chart 3-17 reflected the fact that these two energy forms, which provided 65 per cent of Canada's total energy requirements in 1975, are assumed to contribute smaller shares in the years 2000 and 2025, dropping to 50 and 43 per cent respectively. However, their ability to fulfil this reduced expectation, according to the NEB projections of producibility from known reserves and assumed future discoveries, will fall far short of these lowered allocations. The sheer magnitude of the prospective supply deficit gives some idea of the overwhelming challenge facing the nation. Based on the modest exploration results of the past ten years and the lack of confirmed commercial discoveries, it does not appear likely that the frontier regions will contribute signficant commercial oil and gas reserves to alter this picture materially.

In the LEAP report, electric energy from nuclear power stations was assigned a much larger role for the future, increasing its contribution from 2 per cent of total energy needs in 1975 to 15 per cent by 2000 and to 18 per cent by 2025, in part to substitute for declining oil and gas availability. But such substitution would require a massive transformation in end-use applications, a process that does not appear to have commenced to any great degree. Consequently, as indicated in Chart 4-3, the present Canadian nuclear power program lags far behind the schedule required to achieve the market allocation results called for in the LEAP study.[2]

Even with the reduced nuclear development program of Ontario Hydro, the Ontario Royal Commission on Electric Power Planning found that the "recently approved Ontario Hydro uranium contracts, plus existing export commitments, already more than exhaust Ontario's currently estimated reasonably assured uranium resources in the measured and indicated categories."[3] Since 68 per cent of Canada's presently known uranium reserves in these categories are in Ontario, the current uranium supply outlook does not give confidence that a much larger national nuclear power program such as that envisaged in the LEAP report can be fuelled for long with Canadian uranium resources. Here again, because of the world supply/demand outlook (see Chart 4-1), it would be impractical to count on foreign imports to meet domestic shortages. In view of the uncertainties of the uranium resource question, and regardless of all the other highly contentious issues surrounding nuclear power, it is questionable whether it makes sense to rely on a nuclear generation program of the immense scale recommended in the LEAP report.

Nor does indigenous coal appear to be the salvation to offset declining oil and gas production. Based on our present knowledge of mineable reserves, it does not appear that there are enough large coal surpluses, recoverable at reasonable prices, to manufacture synthetic oil and gas in quantities sufficient to provide a significant substitute for declining conventional petroleum supplies. The LEAP report calls upon coal to increase its contribution to total energy supply to about 2.2 quads of primary energy in the year 2000 and 2.4 quads by 2025, compared with less than 1.0 quad in 1975. While this represents a significantly increased role for coal, the contribution to the gap left by declining oil and gas is modest. In addition, such use of coal would exhaust Canada's currently defined recoverable coal reserves by 2025.

The unquestionable outlook is that a shift from non-renewable to renewable energy sources is essential and that it should get underway as soon as possible. The tar sands and heavy oil deposits are realistic candidates for assisting in a smooth transition. And the health, safety, and environmental aspects of the nuclear option together with the high risks and major uncertainties associated with the successful commercialization of complex new technologies required by the breeder and fusion processes suggest that much greater emphasis be placed in the long-run on renewable sources rather than on advanced nuclear power.

The Dual Challenge for Energy Policy

Monumental efforts will clearly have to be made to avoid the energy supply crises now threatening Canada. Equally clear is the fact that, by themselves, attempts to address this crisis only by bringing on greater supplies of the energy sources we currently depend upon – conventional oil and gas, uranium, and coal – will delay and certainly magnify the crisis. The energy problem Canada faces is not just of petroleum short-

90

ages in the next five to fifteen years; over the next twenty to fifty years, a fundamental shift in Canada's primary sources of energy must be made. The present economic system, which is dependent on non-renewable hydrocarbons, must be modified to operate primarily on sustainable sources of energy. Thus Canada faces two major energy challenges: it must avoid a painful and potentially devastating crisis of energy shortages over the next two decades and beyond; and it must lay the basis for, and make significant steps towards, a sustainable energy future based on non-depleting energy resources.

Any move towards a solution of the inevitable energy crisis of necessity must involve an analysis of past and present policies together with an assessment of their effectiveness. If such policies are found wanting, new ones must be designed to overcome the difficulties facing the nation. The following sections address the question whether Canada's past and current policies can provide an effective response to the dual energy challenge. The first summarizes the main elements of federal oil and gas policy, briefly indicating the results these policies have achieved; the second analyzes the centrepiece of federal energy policy – the "high-price scenario."

Oil and Gas Policy Re-examined

While energy industries in this country are regulated to a considerable extent, in the past Canadians and their governments have relied mainly on the private sector to develop and deliver the energy supplies required by the Canadian economy. Under this system, after an auspicious two decades following the Second World War, the supply outlook for oil and gas has deteriorated continuously since the mid-1960s, and the rate of decline has been accelerated by large exports to the United States. In addition, because the industry is largely foreign controlled, foreign investment and ownership interests have expanded as prices rose and profits increased. This in turn has worsened Canada's balance-of-payments deficits as subsidiaries send dividends and other forms of payment back to their parent companies.[4]

A concomitant policy during the last decade has been to rely on the price mechanism to provide "incentives" to the petroleum industry to perform in a way that would lead to energy self-sufficiency for Canada. Since 1973 industry and governments have combined to put through wellhead price increases for crude oil and natural gas of 400 and 900 per cent, respectively.[5] This policy has been singularly unsuccessful, for despite massive price hikes, the reserves/production ratios have declined steadily and even precipitously. At the same time, in spite of the falling reserves and production levels, as company annual reports reveal, industry profits have shot up. Industry has frequently used the profits from the "incentive" of higher prices to develop even stronger positions in other fields such as coal, uranium, other metals, chemicals or unrelated diversifications or to invest outside of Canada.

Another practice that has developed in relation to the petroleum industry has been to encourage exploration – particularly frontier exploration – through generous allowances and tax credits for individuals and oil companies against taxable income from other sources. Recent reports indicate that because of this policy, the net or after-tax cost of exploratory drilling for an operator in Alberta is 3 cents on each dollar expended; in the Beaufort Sea it is said the net cost of drilling is 9 cents on the dollar; and in Saskatchewan, the net cost can be as high as a credit or saving of 42 cents per dollar expended, or a return of $1.42 for each dollar spent.[6] Some studies suggest that Dome Petroleum operating in the Beaufort Sea probably makes a profit from its exploratory drilling.[7] Despite these liberal arrangements, exploratory footage drilled in northern Canada in both 1978 and 1979 amounted to only 18 per cent of the 1973 level. A large percentage of recent exploratory drilling has been carried out by Petro-Canada and its subsidiary, Panarctic Oils Limited, using mostly federal funds. In fact, less than 1 per cent of the industry's exploration footage drilled in 1978 and 1979 took place in northern Canada.[8] These figures confirm that the private sector has largely withdrawn from the north. They also imply that the petroleum industry does not think highly of the geological prospects in northern Canada, since it could explore there largely at Canadian taxpayers' expense.

Under the National Energy Board, which has authority to approve oil and gas exports to the United States only if the volumes are "surplus to the reasonably foreseeable requirements for use in Canada",[9] this supposed protection of security of supply of both crude oil and natural gas has diminished throughout the 1970s partly as a result of continuing exports (see Charts 3-6 and 3-11). Even though Canadian oil requirements have exceeded domestic producibility since 1975 and remaining conventional reserves have been in apparently irreversible decline since 1969, the NEB has approved a continuation of crude oil exports, albeit on a considerably reduced basis.[10] In 1976, at the industry's urging, it authorized stepped up heavy fuel oil exports. As a result of these actions, by the fall of 1979, there was a serious question whether there would be sufficient heating oil for residents of central and eastern Canada for the oncoming winter. While the nation stayed warm then, the situation will certainly deteriorate with time.

Similarly, even though its own studies forecast future deficits in gas supply, the NEB has not moved to cut back the level of gas exports of approximately one trillion cubic feet per year it approved in 1970 when industry was assuring the nation that reserves were adequate for hundreds of years. Indeed, the Board approved additional gas exports in December 1979 and again in April 1980. In a report, *Canadian Natural Gas Supply and Requirements,* the NEB, by reducing the level of reserves protection for Canadian domestic markets in its mathematical approach to license authorization, laid the groundwork for even larger deliveries to U.S. markets and, ultimately, bigger deficits for Canadians to bear.[11]

All in all, the statute under which the NEB acts has not proven to be much of a stumbling block for industry to surmount in its pursuit of greater exports. Time will tell whether the Board's practices have been adequate relative to its responsibilities. Unfortunately, however, by then it will be too late. At the moment Canada's supply of domestic crude oil is well below current needs and this country can probably expect a natural gas deficiency within five to ten years, if not sooner. Such shortages will have devastating effects.

By contrast, the regulation of oil and gas pipeline charges and earnings on the basis of actual cost has been a successful and consistent thread in Canadian energy policy. As a result, good quality pipeline capacity can meet today's requirements and can be readily expanded if justified by reserves and markets. Pipeline operators, with sound projects, have been able to finance development in a conventional manner. To a large extent they have not relied on or expected their present customers to fund their cash needs. Pipelines have earned good returns for their shareholders.

In comparision with its cost approach for regulating transportation, the government, at the urging of various interests, adopted a "high-price scenario" for oil and gas production that was unrelated to cost. In this scenario natural gas prices were arbitrarily and, for Canadians, expensively tied to those for crude oil at Toronto. As a result, the wellhead prices for crude oil and natural gas have already escalated by 400 and 900 per cent respectively, the bigger percentage increase for gas being a direct consequence of the indexing. The large hikes in retail gas rates moderated growth in domestic demand and, coupled with reduced purchases by U.S. importers because of high Canadian prices – up from 40 cents to $4.47 U.S. in seven years – have generated demands from producers for greater allowable export volumes. Thus one result of the "high-price scenario" will be to deprive Canadians of longer-term natural gas supplies that have been developed with their money – assuming the United States does, in fact, purchase more of the highly priced Canadian supplies. The United States government, justifiably, has protested the mammoth price increases levied by Canada.

Another result of the "high-price scenario" for natural gas is that

Canadian wellhead prices have raced ahead of those in the U.S. There, consumer interests have been partially protected by government price controls in effect for "old" gas discovered prior to 1973. Such gas flowing in interstate commerce is currently (1980) priced at 36 cents per thousand cubic feet, less than 10 per cent of what is paid by Americans for Canadian supplies. While exact comparisons between the two countries are difficult, the weighted average wellhead price for all varieties of gas sold in the United States in 1978, the latest year available, was 89.9 cents per mcf; the comparable figure for Canada was probably about $1.50.[12] Canadian pricing policy has therefore, made natural gas much more expensive for domestic industry, thereby reducing its competitiveness. Residential customers, of course, have also suffered financially as a result of the policy of arbitrarily tying gas prices to those of oil, a policy originally proposed by Imperial Oil Limited in 1973 and adopted by the federal government in 1974.[13]

The federal government also agreed to grant the OPEC "world" price for production from the Suncor and Syncrude tar sands plants to encourage construction of much needed additional facilities in the Athabasca region. But even though both existing plants were authorized by their owners in 1963 and 1972 respectively, when domestic crude oil was about $3 a barrel, federal assurances mean that synthetic oil production would receive over $30 a barrel – the current "world" price.[14]

In May 1980 the federal government indicated it might alter this aspect of pricing policy when the open-ended nature of such a practice dawned upon it. The government had hoped that the high price would provide the incentive for immediate development of tar sand plants. This has not happened. The one new plant proposed – Alsands managed by Shell Canada – remains on the drawing board pending even better financial terms and final approval by the Alberta government. Press reports indicate Shell is holding out for a taxation regime that would allow it to recoup all of its investment before it would be subject to normal taxation and royalties,[15] and Alberta is withholding approval until its pricing demands for conventional oil production are met. Shell Canada earned $151 million in 1978 and paid no current income taxes because of the existing rules regarding capital cost allowances and other generous tax arrangements, but it apparently wants even better "incentives." Alberta's Heritage Trust Fund has grown to $7 billion and is climbing rapidly. From this it is difficult not to conclude that the petroleum industry and the Alberta government, recognizing the vulnerability of the Canadian economy to oil shortages, is seizing the opportunity to exact financial concessions from the federal government and Canadians generally far in excess of what is reasonable or equitable.

As is demonstrated in Chapter 6, Canada needs to develop one

94

125,000 barrels per day synthetic oil plant each year for the next twelve years if the country is to become self-sufficient in petroleum by 1995. While this need must have been obvious to oil executives for many years, the private sector petroleum industry has not launched a new project in the past seven years and has built only one – Syncrude – in the past twelve years. Such performance is obviously inadequate for the task at hand, and must be unacceptable to any knowledgeable federal government.

The issue of resource ownership and the ultimate right of control is another aspect of federal energy policy in need of resolution. The short-lived Conservative government proposed to vest complete authority for the ownership and control of both onshore and offshore resources with provincial governments. And Premier Lougheed of Alberta argues that the provinces have the power to develop or not develop resources and sell or not sell production. Indeed, he exercised such power in 1973–74 when he refused to authorize additional removals of natural gas from Alberta to the provinces east of Alberta until his demand for an approximate fivefold increase in price was met. If this power were to remain unchallenged, energy supplies vital to the welfare of the remainder of the country could be withheld until such demands were satisfied. Control over natural resource development by the provinces must be offset by federal authority to regulate resources essential to the national interest. This suggests a need for a political rather than a legal solution. Recent statements by provincial premiers bent on exclusive control over resources appear to be exactly opposite to the vital needs of the nation as a whole. New Alberta legislation appears aimed at threatening the security of energy supply for the remainder of the country.

A useful exercise in this connection is to compare oil and gas policy with that of electricity. For several decades, responsibility for the assurance of adequate electric energy supplies has resided with the provinces except for the control of exports and imports of electric power and the construction and operation of international power lines.[16]

Provincial control is logical because of the nature of electric energy and the fact that it is uneconomic to transmit over long distances. In all provinces except Alberta, and there it is closely government regulated, the provision of electric power has been taken over or provided by crown agencies. Provincial government guarantees have greatly assisted the financing of the expansion of capacity to meet rapidly growing market requirements. Electric utility systems have responded by timely additions of new generating stations. The relatively assured outlook for future electric energy supplies in Canada is in sharp contrast with the continually deteriorating prospects for oil and gas.

While there are many aspects to this wide discrepancy in prospective reliability, the relative security of electric energy supply can be attributed largely to public rather than the private ownership of the enterprise, and the fact that it is subject to government authority and direction. Another reason for the success is the fact that the industry is domestically rather than foreign controlled; hence it is managed with a markedly different philosophy relative to its responsibilities to the public. A third factor is that it operates on a cost-based approach and does not exploit its monopoly situation in the marketplace, so that its rate increases have been modest and based directly on costs. Some people believe that a similar arrangement should be introduced for the oil and gas industry; in other words, that the ownership and direction of that industry be assumed by government. This idea has considerable merit and should be studied carefully.

The "High-Price Scenario"

In June 1975 the Petroleum Administration Act was passed by Parliament, affirming the federal government's authority to regulate the price of Canadian crude oil and natural gas in interprovincial and export trade. It provided for prices to be fixed by agreement between the federal government and a producing province. However, failing such agreement, it vested federal authorities with the right and responsibility to fix wellhead prices for most of the domestically produced oil and natural gas sold in Canada. The statute clarified an issue of jurisdiction then in dispute between Ottawa and Alberta. Since that time the petroleum industry and Alberta have continued to pressure the government to increase drastically the prices Canadians pay for oil and gas. By January 1980, as illustrated in Charts 3-6 and 3-11, the government had responded with a 400 per cent hike in the domestic wellhead price of crude oil and 900 per cent escalation in the equivalent price of natural gas, despite its avowed intention to fight inflation. In addition, when the even higher price for gas exported to the United States is taken into account, the wellhead price received by gas producers has actually gone up considerably more than 900 per cent.

Faced with rapidly declining life indices for both oil and gas and in spite of already sizable wellhead price rises, *An Energy Strategy for Canada*, a study prepared for the federal government, recommended that Canada adopt a "high-price scenario" for domestically produced hydrocarbon energy.[17] One of the major weaknesses of this particular study was that it covered only the limited period from 1976 to 1990. Notwithstanding this short-term view, it purported to show that after experiencing deficits in the 1980s, Canada would have an overall surplus of energy supplies by 1990 if a "high-price scenario" were adopted. Not surprisingly, based on the arbitrary assumptions of the study, it concluded that a "low-price scenario" would lead to a situation in which only 75 per cent of our energy requirements could be met from domestic sources.

Under the "high-price scenario", it was assumed that the price for domestically produced crude oil would rise to the OPEC "world" price, while the "low-price scenario" assumed Canadian domestic energy prices would stay at their 1975 year-end levels in real terms.[18]

The principal reason for the different result was that under the "high-price scenario" it was assumed that beginning in 1982, huge volumes of frontier natural gas would become available reaching 2 trillion cubic feet annually by 1990; this would not occur under the "low-price scenario." For both scenarios large crude oil deficits were forecast with the shortages being greater in the case of lower prices for domestic production, since it was further assumed that 500,000 barrels per day of frontier oil would emerge under the "high-price scenario" while no comparable development would take place if the lower priced alternative were followed. In short, recoverable petroleum reserves were assumed to be "price elastic," the argument put forward by the oil industry and many economists that unfortunately has not proven to be true.

The study did not indicate whether a two-price system for Canadian oil and gas – one for the low-cost Southern Basin fields and a higher one for possible frontier sources – was ever considered. Nor did it attempt to calculate the windfall profits that would accrue to oil companies and producing provinces from the "high-price scenario" when revenues would far exceed production costs. It did, however, repeat the industry argument that no frontier supplies would be forthcoming under the "low-price scenario," seemingly ignoring that the bulk of hinterland exploration to that date had been done before 1974 when prices were low. The study warned briefly that "higher energy prices will impose direct burdens on energy consumers, could lead to serious structural adjustment problems for certain regions of Canada and particular Canadian industries, and will impose additional costs on all Canadians by increasing the rate of inflation." But that was about the extent of its expressed concern for the adverse economic effects of a policy that to date has added over $200 billion to the ultimate amount Canadians will have to pay for already proven hydrocarbon reserves.

Referring to attempts to determine the effects that increases in oil and natural gas prices would have on the consumer price index (CPI), it concluded that the average impact of a $1.00 per barrel hike in oil prices would increase the CPI by about 1 per cent over a twelve-month period, though it allowed that the estimate might be high. Somewhat ironically, the brief discussion on the possible inflationary effects of large arbitrary increases in oil and gas prices took place when the Anti-Inflation Board (AIB) operated. The AIB was supposed to limit price rises to increases in costs, although for reasons not specified, energy prices were placed outside its jurisdiction.

Still, under the circumstances, it is perhaps understandable but not excusable that the federal government opted for the "high-price scenario." The pressure from the producing provinces and the oil companies to increase petroleum prices much more rapidly than in pre-OPEC days was reinforced by a report by its own officials concluding that high prices for oil and gas would solve the problem of looming shortages, at least until 1990. While the report hedged carefully and pointed out many of the uncertainties in the situation, the data must have looked convincing to the layman politician. Industry had long urged the export of southern Canadian oil and gas because the hydrocarbon potential of the frontier areas was alleged to be tremendous and just waiting to be tapped. Now here was a study that forecast phasing in large volumes of frontier supplies to eliminate energy shortages by 1990. The report also predicted that high prices would dampen energy demand by a significant 7 per cent. But the costs of adopting such a policy have been high for Canadians, especially those on fixed incomes, and the benefits have been negligible.

Clearly, with the exception of the areas of pipeline regulation and electric generation, federal energy policy in recent years has been totally inadequate and mainly adverse to the Canadian public interest. Even though governments have been aware of the declining life indices for Canadian oil and gas reserves for many years, the two major political parties in Canada have continued to rely basically on the private sector oil industry to develop the supplies the country will need in future years. Both political parties have in the past supported policies that give the oil companies huge price increases at the comsumer's expense and generous tax allowances at the taxpayer's expense. How governments, which are supposed to be dedicated to serving the public interest, continue to follow practices that have proven so costly for Canadians and so ineffective in securing future supplies is difficult to understand.

My own view is that today's predicament is primarily a result of the federal government and its advisers accepting industry promises at face value and not being equipped to challenge or question the arguments and presentations of the companies executives, lawyers, accountants, and consultants. After all, if the industry predicted energy self-sufficiency in response to higher prices, who in government knew more than industry experts? While some might have recognized their statements as self-serving, probably no individual was prepared to question seriously their logic. As a consequence, the country with substantial energy potential faces serious economic problems resulting from pending energy shortages of probably unmanageable proportions.

The Costs

The absence of a two-price system that would protect Canadian industry and consumers from increases for oil supplies discovered and developed when costs were low has meant that Canadians have faced excessive price hikes and the established producing companies have reaped huge profit increases. Despite this, the government in late 1979 proposed to more than double the size of the wellhead price increases to be paid by users of crude oil to $4.00 per year in 1980 and to $4.50 per barrel in each of 1981, 1982, and 1983. By 1984, the average price of a barrel of domestic oil would have been over $34 compared with $14.75 in January 1980, and about $3.00 in January 1973.[19] Presumably, natural gas prices, indexed to the wellhead price of oil since 1974, would have escalated in lock step and would have averaged about $5.25 in 1984 compared with 17 cents in 1973. It is difficult to comprehend how federal policy-makers could propose such severe price increases for energy commodities essential to everyday living.

One effect of government policy has been to greatly increase producing company profits. For example, the after tax-income of Hudson's Bay Oil and Gas Company Limited, a producing rather than an integrated oil company, escalated from $28 million in 1972 to $107 million in 1978 despite a 32 per cent drop in net production of oil and gas during the interval.[20] In 1979 HBOG's annual profit increased further to $132 million with production up 8 per cent. Another producer, Amoco Canada Petroleum Company, experienced a profit increase from $51 million in 1973 to $140 million in 1979. Production volumes are not known, but they were probably significantly lower in the latter year than in 1973. An example of an integrated oil company is Imperial Oil Limited, the largest in the industry and a subsidiary of Exxon Corporation. Imperial's after tax income increased from $153 million in 1972 to $471 million in 1979. After-tax profits for the first six months of 1980 were $300 million compared with $197 million in the same period in 1979. On a country-wide basis, from 1972 through 1979, arbitrary wellhead price increases for oil and gas legislated by the federal government have cost Canadians an extra $30 billion over 1973 price levels. Chart 5-1 shows that in 1979 alone Canadian consumers paid $9 billion more for the wellhead component of the petroleum products and natural gas than if pre-OPEC prices had remained in effect.[21]

CHART 5-1
COST TO CANADIAN CONSUMERS OF
OIL & GAS PRICE INCREASES, 1973–79

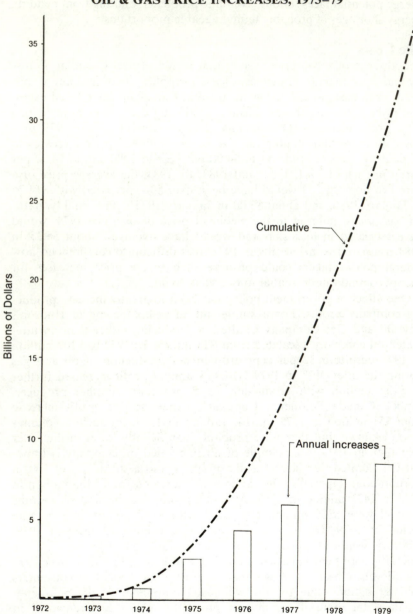

The additional price paid by Canadians to the oil industry and various governments – mainly Alberta – would have skyrocketed under the aborted 1979 proposal to $24 billion in 1982 and $36 billion in 1984. As can be seen in Chart 5-1, the cumulative effect of the oil and gas price increases is alarming. If the federal government acquiesces to Alberta's demand that Canadians be charged prices for domestic production equivalent to those negotiated by the Clark and Lougheed governments, the total effect would be to add another $350 billion to the selling price of the existing 18 billion barrel inventory of oil and gas reserves (see Chart 3-16) over and above the $200 billion resulting from increases between 1973 and 1980. Indeed, the dollar amounts are so large that it is impossible to forecast precisely their impact on the national economy or on the welfare of individuals.

The Liberal government's present commitment to a "blended" domestic oil price based on actual costs of both domestic production and foreign imports would result in a lower than "world" price for oil. In addition, the throne speech of April 1980 promised

- a Petroleum Price Auditing Agency to investigate and report on oil company costs, profits, capital expenditures, and ownership;
- a bigger budget for Petro-Canada;
- early construction of a gas pipeline from Montreal to the maritime provinces;
- more stringent standards for automobiles to encourage conservation; and
- 50 per cent ownership of the Canadian petroleum industry by 1990 as a result of unspecified government programs.

All of this represents steps in the right direction. However, taken together, the various initiatives do not come to grips with the alarming energy supply deficits confronting the nation.

Clearly, too, in Canada as in the United States, energy cost increases have contributed substantially to the rise in the inflation rate. Chart 5-2 shows that the acceleration in the inflation rate coincided with the rapid increase in oil and gas prices in the mid 1970s and that, despite the efforts of the Anti-Inflation Board to control factors other than energy and food prices in the 1976–78 period, it remained around 9 per cent. Accompanying this increase have been substantial increases in living costs for all consumers. Hardest hit have been the low-income Canadians and those on fixed incomes. In addition, savings of Canadians are being eroded.

At the same time, energy price increases have added tremendously to the profits of the producing companies, most of which are not Canadian; increased the level of foreign ownership and control of Canadian resources; and aggravated our balance-of-payments problem and weakened the Canadian dollar because of the higher annual outflows of dividends to parent companies. To date the high-price policy has resulted in a transfer of $30 billion from Canadian consumers to the petroleum industry, the Alberta government, and the federal government.

But this is a small amount compared with the more than $500 billion extra consumers will pay in the future for today's proved reserves. That amount would go to the industry and governments if the Canadian domestic price is increased to the present "world" level of over $30 per barrel. Thus the costs of the "high-price scenario" have been steep. The question that needs to be examined is what Canadians have gained from this policy.

The Alleged Benefits

Three main arguments are put forward in favour of going to the world price for oil and gas. First, the argument is made that Canadian energy prices must go to "world" levels in the interests of energy conservation. But while it is obvious that enormous price rises will force some reductions to take place, there is no evidence to support the proposition that current world prices will be sufficient to achieve the necessary demand decreases. In Canada and elsewhere, energy consumption has continued to increase, despite the huge price rises since 1973.[22] Other measures, such as rationing and allocation, can be much more effective in achieving lower consumption levels and much less inequitable. Rationing by means of price is cruel and oppressive, particularly for the poor, and unduly rewarding to those who control the sources of supply.

Second, some argue that higher domestic oil prices are needed in order to reduce the expenses of the federal treasury for the oil import compensation program, the payments made by the federal government to the oil companies in order to achieve equalized costs for crude oil across the country. While there is some merit to this argument, it does not make sense to levy an additional burden on Canadians of $20 billion per year in order to save the federal government $1.6 billion.[23] Other more efficient and logical methods could be used to tackle this problem, such as an excise tax on present consumption of petroleum products, a "blended" nation-wide average price, or perhaps an excess profits tax on domestic production earnings. In reality, this particular problem would not have arisen if effective long-term energy policies for the management of Canada's petroleum resources had been instituted years ago, but now that this problem is here, it has to be dealt with until it is overcome.

102

CHART 5-2
ANNUAL RATE OF INFLATION, CANADA, 1967–79

Per cent

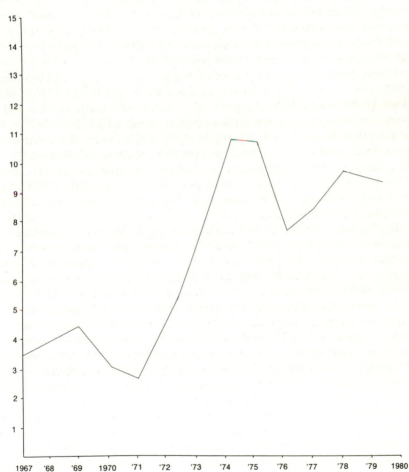

Source: A.E. Ames and Co., Strategy (Summer 1979), p. 4.

Third, the argument that appears to have been the main motivation for government policy is that the higher prices would bring further energy supplies on stream. Ever since 1973, when the Canadian petroleum industry first acknowledged that an energy supply problem existed, the solution urged upon governments for the avoidance of future shortages was to increase the price of existing production. Studies purported to show that high prices would bring on large increases in hydrocarbon reserves.[24] Governments blindly accepted the argument that oil and gas supplies were indeed price elastic. In spite of its being largely discredited, industry continues to use the same argument with great success financially.[25] But can price increases bring forth significant new reserves and provide the necessary and sufficient impetus for Canada to shift to other sources of energy supply?

Under federal government control, the price of a barrel of Canadian crude rose to $14.75 per barrel on January 1, 1980 (see Chart 3-6). Between 1950 and 1970 the price of a barrel of Saudi Arabian light crude oil FOB the Persian Gulf varied between $1.75 and $2.08 U.S. and in 1970 it stood at $1.80. In the early 1970s under the control of the OPEC cartel, it began to edge upwards, reaching $2.48 by 1973.[26] In a series of drastic price increases, OPEC raised its prices to a level 1500 per cent higher than its 1970 price by June of 1980. OPEC has been able to make these prices stick because the importing nations have no alternatives.

In the years before OPEC made such high demands, the price of petroleum-based energy in Canada bore some relationship to the cost of finding, developing, and producing the reserves. Indeed, the Canadian petroleum industry was quite profitable in 1972 when oil was priced at $2.85 per barrel and natural gas at 17 cents per Mcf. After 1973, however, profits rose substantially. As Chart 5-3 shows, producing industry gross revenues increased between 1973 and 1978 from $3,037 million to $10,422 million, even though production volumes fell by 19 per cent during the interval.[27] Total after-tax industry profits or dividends paid to parent companies are impossible to ascertain since many companies, wholly owned subsidiaries of foreign corporations, do not report publicly on their Canadian operations. However, the Chart gives some indication of the magnitude of the profit increases the industry has received as a result of the large-scale hikes in wellhead prices. Also shown is the amount paid in royalties, primarily to governments. Royalty payments rose 600 per cent, from $481 million in 1973 to $3,383 million in 1978, despite the drop in production. This amount, which is the principal source of revenue for the Alberta Heritage Trust Fund, has been provided by consumers through their purchases of petroleum products and natural gas.

CHART 5-3
PRODUCING INDUSTRY COSTS AND REVENUES, CANADA, 1973-78

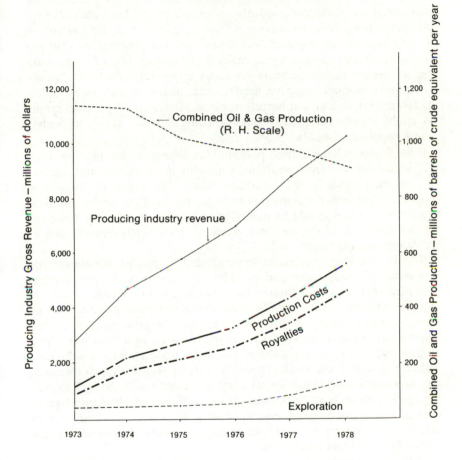

Source: CPA Reserves Committee
Oilweek Magazine

Despite the huge price increases, the thesis that the "high-price scenario" would result in frontier discoveries that would be contributing 500,000 barrels per day of crude oil and 2 trillion cubic feet of natural gas annually to gas supply well before 1990 is not being borne out. Exploratory drilling footage in the north has fallen 82 per cent since 1973. While because of the fragmentary nature of the information and the physical and environmental hazards of the area, no conclusions can be drawn about whether northern Canada has any real potential for commercial oil production, industry response to the land auction suggests very strongly that the answer is "no". Exploratory drilling results in the past year off the coast of Newfoundland have been somewhat encouraging, though the scant information released to date or even available to insiders makes accurate estimates impossible. Tentative "possible" reserve estimates suggests the Hibernia discovery may be a moderate 500 million to 2 billion barrels in place. Assuming 35 per cent recovery might be achievable, this would be equivalent to a three- to twelve-month supply for Canada.[28]

If the frontiers have limited potential, as appears to be the case, then the "high-price scenario" really only benefits those owners and holders of producing rights in the Southern Basin. The vision of huge new supplies from frontier regions that industry has held out as the justification for high prices should be dispelled in favour of realistic policies for the development, in the national interest, of known resources such as the Athabasca Tar Sands.

Nor has the high-price scenario succeeded to date in stimulating the emergence of energy alternatives. The vast commercial opportunities presented by such circumstances have not resulted in a rush of activity by firms wishing to get in on the ground floor of the renewable energy business. The reasons for this are many, but the principal one is that investors are unlikely to want to become involved in a situation where an essential lower cost commodity has to be replaced with a substitute higher cost one of uncertain capability. Private sector investors want to bet on a sure moneymaker or, at least, the closest they can get to one. And governments have responded to the difficulty of obtaining significant private sector participation in renewable energy developments by granting still larger price increases to the producers of non-renewables, primarily the oil and gas companies.

This study recommends a cost-based approach to energy pricing, with cost to include reasonable royalties on the production of non-renewable resources and an appropriate return on investor-contributed capital. Thus oil, natural gas, and coal would be priced in similar fashion to electric energy. Such an approach would eliminate windfall profits, profiteering, and overcharging for essential commodities. Cost-based prices could be augmented by the addition of excise taxes if such were considered desirable to fund new energy supply projects or for other purposes deemed to be in the national interest. There would be many benefits in such an approach.

Conclusion

Under the "high-price scenario" Canadian consumers have contributed $30 billion to the petroleum industry and various governments in 1974–79 period through government legislated price increases. But despite these massive payments, the energy supply outlook is worse than it was five and ten years ago. Essentially nothing is taking place to facilitate the efficient transfer of energy demands from non-renewable to renewable sources on a timetable that will dovetail with the exhaustion of the former.

Further, we can no longer assume, if we ever could, that modern technology will come to the rescue in the approaching energy crises, an argument advanced by those who advocate exploitation of natural resources at maximum rates. The U.S. experience of ten or more years of declining oil and gas reserves and increased dependency on foreign imports stands as eloquent testimony to the fact that the most technologically advanced nation in the world has been powerless to counter its growing domestic energy supply deficits.

Such a situation dramatically underlines the fact that the main difficulty with relying on the price mechanism to provide essential future supplies is that there is absolutely no assurance that it will work. There is nothing to stop the private sector beneficiaries of the high prices from taking their money and doing with it as they please. Indeed, this is already happening. Individual oil companies are taking their greatly enlarged cash flows and investing not just in energy related areas such as coal properties and uranium but in nonferrous metal mines, chemical plants, real estate, and other unrelated activities. As well as diverting funds from the needed investments in renewable energy, a continuation of this practice will make these entities even more dominant on the Canadian scene, where they already control key industrial sectors. Their special interests do not coincide with the need for assured energy supplies for Canadians in the future. Life indices for oil and gas continue to decline while prices and profits escalate.

One of the difficult questions facing the government of Canada is how it should structure its efforts to meet its goal of energy self-sufficiency. Clearly, energy pricing policies must be formulated that are geared to the true cost of developing resources, not ones based on such vague and open-ended concepts as "world" oil prices. Comprehensive, co-ordinated, and co-operative effort is required from governments, the oil and gas industries, manufacturing industries, financial institutions, and the educational systems in order to develop hydrocarbon resources now largely lying idle. Only by mobilizing the major human, physical and institutional resources of the country in a carefully co-ordinated manner can what President Carter in 1977 properly described for the U.S. as the "moral equivalent of war" be urgently and effectively waged in Canada.

While the outlook for the future is alarming, it should not be regarded as hopeless. Now is the time to build on our strengths and work our way around our weaknesses. The federal government must understand the seriousness of the situation facing Canada and be willing to tackle the problems on a vigorous and intelligent basis. The argument that it should not interfere with the "market system" or the private sector is no substitute for comprehensive policy. Indeed, the best way to ensure that adequate energy supplies are available is to develop a system whereby the large sums Canadians now have to pay for current domestic energy production are channeled directly into productive investment in both non-renewable and renewable sources. In this way both consumers and governments would be assured that the capital being contributed through high prices for low-cost production was being utilized most effectively. Such a prospect is examined in Chapter 6.

A National Energy Policy

The analysis in the preceeding chapters points to the unalterable fact that if the challenge to find an effective energy policy for Canada is to be met, a fresh approach based on sound fundamentals is required. Both the threat of imminent energy shortages and the necessity for the transition to a sustainable energy future call clearly for the creation of a comprehensive national energy policy directed specifically at tackling these tasks. Such an overall policy must have two basic objectives. First, it must seek to eliminate, or at least minimize, the prospective short- and medium-term energy shortages through a co-ordinated, two-pronged effort to improve the supply outlook and to decrease unnecessary energy demand. Second, the policy must provide Canada with a sustainable energy base over the longer term. These goals cannot, however, be pursued without regard for the manner in which they are achieved, and the following principles must guide the effort to attain the dual objectives.

Guiding Principles

The first principle is that the policy must lead to energy self-sufficiency for Canada. Having in mind the sizable energy resource base of the nation and the high degree of uncertainty associated with foreign supplies as well as their price, it would be unsound to leave any part of the country dependent on energy imports. Of course, the attainment of self-sufficiency requires a focus not only on the development of new supplies but also on a reduction in demand through conservation.

The second principle is that energy developments should assist in solving other Canadian problems such as unemployment, regional disparities, and adverse trade balances. For example, machinery and equipment required for new energy supply projects should be designed and fabricated in Canada, thereby enlarging the country's manufacturing capability and ensuring maximum employment opportunities in regions where improvement is needed. Optimum energy prices along with reliable supplies will serve to attract stable employment opportunities for the Canadian work force. In this way the process of solving Canada's energy problems would serve as a foundation for future national economic growth.

The third principle is that the policy must be fair and equitable for all Canadians. The interests of one area or one group should not be allowed to take precedence over those of the others. For example, investors should earn a reasonable return, but profiteering should not be permitted; ownership rights should be recognized, but royalty rates should not be excessive; and the rights of native people and minority groups should be preserved, while the needs of the majority are met. The likely socioeconomic effects of new development projects should also be ascertained and considered in the planning process.

The fourth principle is that the policy guard and respect the environment. New projects should be undertaken only after their safety and environmental effects are carefully assessed and accepted.

The fifth principle is that Canadian ownership and control of industry should be maximized so that the benefits flowing from natural resource development accrue to Canadians rather than to foreign interests. Growth in foreign ownership should be reversed in order to reduce future balance-of-payment deficits.

The sixth principle is that the policy must be consistent yet flexible. New plans and modifications to old ones should be logical, reasonably predictable to entrepreneurs, and equitable to all concerned. It should not reflect a "beggar thy neighbour" philosophy.

Some of the more immediate and specific policy objectives should be to attain energy self-sufficiency by 1995, the earliest date that is realistic, and to eliminate the vulnerability of Quebec and Atlantic Canada to offshore oil embargoes and other supply interruptions; maintain total energy supplies and prices at levels designed to ensure overall satisfactory national economic performance and to remove excessive profits from energy pricing; lower foreign investment in the economy and control of the petroleum industry from the present level of about 80 per cent to 25 per cent by 1990 by managing new energy supply projects to ensure maximum Canadian ownership as well as the highest domestic content in engineering, construction, and equipment manufacturing; and use energy developments to lessen regional economic imbalances, wherever feasible.

But what is required to implement a policy based on these principles and objectives? What is the relationship between government and the private sector that is necessary to bring about the required changes? Can the private sector undertake the necessary overall planning?

110

Government and the Private Sector

The precise nature of the role of the government and the private sector in the energy arena may be difficult to define. However, one thing is quite clear. The private sector, left to its own or with minimal intervention from government, is incapable of meeting the challenges of Canadian energy policy. The private sector has an essential role to play in developing many of the resources needed to overcome the anticipated supply shortages and in moving Canada to a sustainable energy future. But the lead, overall direction, co-ordination, and planning must come from the senior government for two major reasons.

The first reason stems from the fact that the choices that are made about energy supply and demand have profound social and political implications that must be dealt with explicitly and satisfactorily; the need for energy security to be met through energy self-sufficiency and the concerns for equity, human safety, the environment, and industrial development are all embodiments of the pervasiveness of energy policy. In addition, a special dimension of concern for the future is contained in the objective of a sustainable energy future, as was recently summed up by the Ontario Royal Commission on Electric Power Planning: "Consciousness of the welfare of future generations should be the central criterion in the evaluations of energy options."[1]

On its own, the private sector is simply not capable of taking adequate account of these social implications. Its objectives are only episodically and coincidently harmonious with the needs of the entire country and its citizens. Under a "market" system that allocates production on the basis of price, vital supplies might go to the highest bidder, which might well be the least desirable result; for example, scarce petroleum reserves might be used for export or for pleasure boats rather than essential pharmaceuticals. The traditional goals of businessmen are to maximize profits, raise the market price of their companies' shares, and improve their own compensation and perquisites. Their perspective tends to be short term; their horizon the balance sheet. The objectives of foreign-controlled and Canadian-owned firms have been to find, exploit, and export indigenous natural resources as expeditiously as possible. The consequences for the country of perpetuating such behaviour in the energy sector will be dire.

The second major reason that the private sector is incapable of taking the lead in responding to the energy challenges is logistical. Across-the-board planning and co-ordination of the supply of and demand for the entire spectrum of energy forms – from oil and gas to coal, uranium, and renewables – is basic to tackling the issues and problems. No single company or industry has the scope of knowledge, activity, and authority required to tackle the planning function, let alone the total job.

The perspective and co-ordination required to meet the two objectives, as well as the nature of some of the tasks, demand government leadership for several crucial reasons. As supplies of key energy forms dwindle, remaining production will have to be allocated to essential uses that serve the national interest, as defined by government. Tough and unpleasant decisions for individual consumers will also be required, limiting their choice or access to what may be preferred forms of energy. Evenhanded administration of vital but diminishing resources will require new legislation and regulations that can only be promulgated and enforced by governments.

Any overall program designed to head off the paralysing energy shortages facing the country will have to involve the mobilization of national resources – manpower, manufacturing, educational systems, natural resources, and financial institutions – that can only be achieved by governments and industry working together co-operatively. It is unrealistic to believe that industry on its own can provide comprehensive solutions. As has been seen, a major energy supply project, the Alaska Highway gas pipeline, has been unable to go forward under industry sponsorship; yet James Bay, under government auspices, has been developed essentially on schedule.

In Canada, exercising control over the petroleum industry in the national interest is difficult because of the high degree of foreign ownership. Subsidiary company managements must serve the financial interests of their parent companies, which stress the export of Canada's diminishing supplies to increase revenues and to help meet U.S. energy shortages. Indeed, whenever a spot excess of producibility over demand appears, the industry immediately applies to ship it to the United States.

But a major, leading role for government does not mean the emasculation of the private sector; rather, the reverse would be true. The private sector would benefit enormously from providing the essential services required for the successful implementation of the national energy policy. For example, projects aimed at bringing on stream new non-conventional oil, coal, nuclear, and renewable energy supplies will require the expenditure of millions of man-days in the design, engineering, construction, and equipment manufacturing phases. The opportunities for the private sector in supplying services and equipment will be great indeed. Major new corporations will be required to operate additional facilities; existing entities will have to be expanded.

While Canadian ownership and control of key sectors of the economy have suffered as a result of being next to a dominant and wealthy neighbour, the favourable aspect of the foreign ownership issue is that many Canadian nationals have gained experienced in managerial and technical processes that otherwise might not have been undertaken in this country. Now is the time to utilize that training and experience by creating or expanding Canadian-owned enterprises directed towards helping solve the energy crisis that is upon us.

An overall energy plan co-ordinating – to the extent necessary to achieve the key objectives and in keeping with essential principles – both demand and supply must be devised by governments presumably with the private sector playing an essential supportive role. What policy elements will bring this about?

The Necessary Policies
In order to meet the challenges embodied in the need for an effective national energy policy, it is apparent that practices very different from those presently in effect will be required during the next ten years. But while broad policies and directions can be outlined here, it would be highly speculative to suggest at this time what detailed policies might be appropriate. Much more work and analysis is required. By 1990, Canada should have an improved understanding of its own and the world's economically recoverable energy resources. If the amounts vary appreciably from today's estimates, or if significant technological breakthroughs have occurred, then obviously such developments should be reflected in policy modifications. Indeed, energy policy should be under constant review to ensure that it responds appropriately to changing circumstances and national and international needs. Unconsidered adherence to past policy and practices for whatever reason should be avoided. This section cites some of the requisites of a new energy policy.

- A prime objective of a fresh approach to energy policy would be to ensure adequacy of future energy supplies through a positive program of new projects aimed at both increased energy conservation and the provision of renewable and non-renewable energy supplies, utilizing an optimum mix of public and private sector capabilities. Federal initiatives should be undertaken to design and implement a national energy supply plan based on known and economically available non-renewable and renewable resources. Substantially improved energy supplies in the 1980s could lead potentially to energy self-sufficiency by 1995 and contribute to reduced balance-of-payments deficits, lowered unemployment rates, and stronger economic performance as a result of perceived energy security.

113

- In any new policy, energy prices should be based on the cost of current production, including reasonable royalties for lessors of non-renewable resources and equitable returns on risk investment. If appropriate, excise taxes or other levies could be added to achieve uniform regional energy prices or funding for new energy supply projects. Such a policy would involve abandoning the "high-price scenario" presently being followed. Under such a scheme, Canadian petroleum product prices would reflect the true cost of developing and delivering hydrocarbon energy, the excessive profit component having been eliminated from domestic supplies. Compared with the present system, this would benefit Canadian manufacturers and would be fair to consumers. Canadian energy prices should then be appreciably lower than those in the United States, although since per capita needs are higher in Canada, total individual energy costs might well be greater in this country. A principal benefit would be that essential synthetic oil plants could go forward with the assurance that production would be sold at a price related to the costs actually incurred, eliminating the argument that still higher prices and lower taxes are needed for tar sands mining production because of the financial risks incurred by the operator. An assured rate of return, after operating costs and royalties were met, would enable the private sector or crown companies to proceed with development plans using conventional financing techniques in the same manner that electricity generating stations are funded.

- A cost-based approach would also imply recognition that the OPEC world price is totally unrelated to costs or to what is fair and equitable for Canadians to pay for their own resources. This would follow similar policies in other oil-producing nations in which their own citizens are not charged the cartel export price. For example, Mexico's domestic gasoline price is about 60 cents per gallon, and in recent legislation Mexico authorized even lower hydrocarbon prices for firms locating in certain designated areas as a catalyst for industrial development. Companies operating new facilities may now benefit from a 30 per cent reduction in the prevailing domestic price for electricity, natural gas, fuel oil, and selected primary petrochemicals.[2] Similarly, gasoline prices in Venezuela are in the 40 to 50 per cents per gallon range, and in Kuwait a gallon of gasoline costs 23 cents.[3] These nations do not handicap their own citizens or industries with burdensome energy prices. The major difference, of course, is that these countries have ejected the international oil companies and now control the development of their energy resources in their own national interest.

- To develop an increased domestic presence in the Canadian petroleum industry, a new energy policy should ensure that the ownership benefits from successful frontier exploration go to those who finance the effort. If exploration is funded by Canadian taxpayers through tax credits and allowances for the industry, the producing rights and profits therefrom should accrue to them. The oil companies would be paid a fee for their services as contractors. Such a scheme would provide the taxpayer with equity and eliminate or reduce monopoly in the petroleum industry. Bidding for frontier work would become more competitive and the dominant position of the major multinationals would gradually be reduced.
- An energy policy to ensure adequate supplies in Canada now and well into the future would permit oil and gas exports only when proved reserves were surplus to at least the twenty-five year needs of the country. Since Canada now does not have hydrocarbon supplies anywhere near this magnitude, present exports should be phased out. In a world of growing uncertainty, such a policy, coupled with a cost-based approach, would hold out the promise of adequate energy supplies at reasonable prices. Canada would then be regarded as a country in which its resources would be available to residents, accomplishing on a national scale what Alberta is currently achieving provincially with its policies of priority access to its oil and gas for Alberta-based operations. If successful, such a policy would help maintain reasonable domestic energy prices and avoid the price gouging that often accompanies shortages. This kind of policy would also foster maximum upgrading of resources prior to export, thereby increasing domestic employment opportunities and aiding economic activity.
- A revised energy policy for Canada should continue to place regulation of interprovincial oil and gas pipelines under federal control. It should also continue to assign responsibility for the assurance of adequate electric energy supplies and the regulation of rates for service basically with the provincies. Federal control of exports and imports of electric power and the construction and operation of international power lines would be maintained. The feasibility of developing a high capacity country-wide electric grid system for the maximum effective national utilization of renewable hydro-electric power could also be examined and, if practical, such a system could be brought into being on a basis somewhat similar to that used for the creation of the Trans-Canada Highway.

As fossil fuels are depleted, the nation will have to look more and more to the transfer of energy demands now served by hydrocarbons to other energy forms. The choices and alternatives must be studied well in advance of such transfers because of the long lead times required for preparation. If Canada is to solve its energy problems in an efficient and intelligent manner, close co-operation between federal and provincial authorities will be required to effect the multiplicity of transitions and transactions the future will entail. But the present political subdivisions create unnecessary and debilitating conflicts that frustrate the development of sound and equitable national plans. The obvious logical solution would be to provide federal authorities with the organizational and operating entities that will endow the senior government with the means of discharging its responsibilities to the nation as a whole.

National Needs Versus Provincial Rights
The British North America Act gave the provinces ownership of natural resources that are on or lie under the ground together with the right to tax them. The same statute gives the federal government jurisdiction over control and regulation of interprovincial and international trade including setting prices for commodities such as oil and gas moving in interprovincial and international commerce. This split jurisdiction is one of the principal stumbling blocks to reaching concensus in Canada on the development of energy resources in a way that will serve the overall national interest.

Alberta, where most of the country's oil and gas deposits appear to exist, has taken a hard line with the rest of Canada on both energy pricing and sharing its resources, over which it was given control by Ottawa in 1930. In 1973–74 Alberta withheld additional volumes of natural gas from the provinces east of Alberta until its pricing demands were met. Partly as a result of great pressure from the Alberta government, the federal government by 1980 had raised the wellhead price of oil by approximately 400 per cent and that for natural gas by 900 per cent over 1973 prices. Increases for both commodities have been highly inflationary and have resulted in massive transfers of capital from the consuming regions to Alberta.

Federal policy has been to make major concessions to the pressures from Alberta. But at the same time, Alberta's Premier Lougheed continues to exhibit little flexibility in his monetary demands. At the premier's conference held in Quebec in August 1979, he responded to a proposal by Premier Davis of Ontario for new federal control of Canadian oil and gas revenues with a fourteen-point attack, item three of which stated: "With the ownership of natural resources implicitly goes the right of a province to decide how to develop its natural resources, how to produce its natural resources, when to produce its natural resources, and whether or not to sell its natural resources."[4]

116

It is clear from this statement that unless Alberta's continuing demands are met, it believes it could restrict or shut off completely the flow of oil and gas to other provinces. This would be intolerable for Canada. Energy supply is vital. The federal government must face up to the realities of the situation and if it is unable to work out a national arrangement with Alberta that is fair for the citizens of the country as a whole, then it must act to bring oil and gas resources under federal jurisdiction as was done many years ago with uranium.

A good illustration of the dangers inherent in the present situation was given in Charts 3-12 and 3-13 prepared by the AERCB, which demonstrate that natural gas shortages will likely start to occur between 1985 and 1992 and will grow in intensity. With Alberta's own thirty-year protection policy in operation, there will be insufficient gas reserves to meet any of the natural gas requirements of the provinces east of Alberta after 2000.

This situation would undoubtedly be totally unacceptable for the federal government of the day. No responsible national government could put up with provincial policies that meant that the citizens of one province would enjoy fully adequate supplies of an essential energy form, while residents of the other provinces were left in the cold. Yet this would be the inevitable outcome if the present Alberta protection policy is allowed to persist. The fact that the Alberta protection period was changed in 1979 from thirty years to twenty-five years does not affect the principle of the situation at all, only some of the details.

Few federal legislators seem to appreciate the current precarious energy balance and the outlook for the future. Studies and reports of Energy, Mines and Resources Canada, such as *An Energy Policy for Canada, An Energy Strategy for Canada*, and *Energy Futures for Canadians*, and the reports of the National Energy Board either mask the severity of the problem or fail to deal with it in a comprehensive way.[5] Similarly, annual reports of the oil and gas companies avoid a hard look at the declining life indices for vital resources, since their interest might well be undermined by public understanding of the impending shortages.

In light of this lack of knowledge and information, it is perhaps not surprising that the important ramifications of the federal-provincial constitutional question as it relates to energy have not been resolved. Either the true magnitude of the energy problems facing the nation has not been perceived by the lawmakers or else they have been hoping a miracle solution will come along, perhaps in the form of massive new hydrocarbon discoveries in accessible locations. Unfortunately, time, geology and geography are not on the side of those who are responsible for analysing Canada's energy dilemma and ensuring solutions. The constitutional issue is one of the present roadblocks that needs to be dealt with expeditiously. Alberta is entitled to reasonable royalties for its oil and gas production, but it must not be allowed to hold the country to ransom or to hoard essential supplies.

Professor Ian McDougall, Osgoode Hall Law School, York University, and an expert in constitutional law, particularly as it applies to resource developments, has commented at length on the constitutional and legal questions involved in bringing energy resources under federal jurisdiction:

> Recent jurisprudence would suggest a rather wide degree of control lies with the federal government over energy development in Canada. The recent *CIGOL* and *Central Canada Potash* cases decided by the Supreme Court suggested a substantially wider federal power under Trade and Commerce and interprovincial trade than was previously thought to be the case. As a result of both decisions it would seem that provinces cannot restrain interprovincial movement of primary resources through either provincial royalties or production pro-rationing. In result, the scope that exists for the federal government under this jursidictional head would appear to be sweeping in the sense that it alone would appear to have the power to set up comprehensive marketing arrangements for interprovincial primary resource flows.
>
> Likewise, under the residuary powers of peace, order and good government the federal authority has a substantial measure of leverage over the energy resource question. The exercise of peace, order and good government as a constitutional justification for federal legislation is virtually unassailable under conditions of emergency. Over and above emergency conditions it would appear quite possible that the residuary power can be employed whenever there exists a substantial national dimension that can alone be addressed by the federal government. Such a dimension can clearly be said to exist with respect to the management of vital energy supplies under conditions of imminent scarcity in a country with a climate as hostile as Canada's. The dependence of national populations, vitally important domestic industries, and indeed the entire capacity of the nation to maintain living standards would seem to qualify federal intervention in a constitutional sense.
>
> Finally, specific legislative jurisdiction can be obtained over some energy resource developments through s.92(10)(c) of the British North America Act which allows for unilateral declarations by the federal government that specific works are to the general advantage of Canada. Such declared works then become subject to federal regulation, even though the proprietary interest remains in its original hands. Thus for example a federal declaration that existing pipelines fell under Canadian jursidiction would not alter the present ownership structure but would clearly make such facilities liable to federal regulation exclusive of provincial control. Carrying on with this example, federal jurisdiction over pipelines would provide the federal government with de facto control over all oil and gas production.[6]

Both federal and provincial governments must seriously endeavour to sort out the current impasse, negotiating an agreement acceptable to both that recognizes the human dimensions of the issues. Only if all other avenues are exhausted should the federal government move unilaterally to impose a solution. The essential feature of the necessary new relationship would be to permit the creation and implementation of an effective and equitable energy policy for the nation as a whole. This does not necessarily imply a huge bureaucracy running all energy supply projects from a single location in Canada; to the maximum extent feasible the construction and operation of physical facilities would be delegated and run under local or regional autonomy. However, overall planning, study of alternatives, pricing policies, and allocation of resources would have to be brought together in order to achieve national objectives on a co-ordinated basis. Such detailed planning would require submissions and recommendations from all regions and constituencies of the nation as well as every branch of the energy industry. But first, clear, logical, and unmistakable lines of political authority and jurisdiction would have to be agreed upon and established.

A National Energy Corporation
In the face of increases in demand for and the declining life indices of non-renewable energy supplies, continuing exponential growth in energy use is not sustainable. In the long term the Canadian economy will have to depend upon renewable energy forms, though a limited amount of time exists during which a somewhat painful but manageable transition away from non-renewables appears possible if appropriate policies and plans are adopted immediately. But it is not logical to expect a foreign-controlled industry, whose primary goal is to maximize profits and to manage affairs for its own advantage, should be given the responsibility for ensuring that Canadian energy supplies will at all times be adequate for future needs and available at reasonable prices. Past reliance by governments and consumers on the private sector oil industry has led to excessive oil and gas exports and today's great uncertainty about the adequacy of oil supplies for the immediate future. Further, while competitive forces may have acted to keep prices reasonable prior to the 1970s, this obviously is no longer the case as control over most energy supply is now concentrated in the major corporations and the producing provinces. To aggravate the problem, the oil and gas companies are quietly moving towards hegemony over the entire energy business by extending their interests into coal, uranium, and even solar power.[7]

Since Canadians will ultimately be dependent solely on renewable energy, the sooner this is recognized by those responsible for the future welfare of the nation the better. It is essential to start planning now, though in some respects it may be already too late in view of the rapidly widening deficit between crude oil requirements and domestic production. This situation will only get worse with time. Still, a belated attempt to undertake energy supply planning is better than no action at all.

Not only must new energy supplies be brought on stream rapidly but difficult decisions about how to manage demand are upon us. How are the dwindling supplies of crude oil to be allocated? What will be an equitable distribution of domestic crude when the next offshore oil supply interruption hits central and eastern Canada? How can the present 45 per cent of total energy dependence on petroleum products be reduced to a level that can be sustained? Clearly, these are national problems. Such difficult questions must be tackled at the national level if evenhanded solutions are to be achieved.

Also, as society becomes more complex, careful attention must be given to the proper level of government at which various problems and issues can best be addressed. The framers of the British North America Act 113 years ago could not in their wildest imaginations have visualized the complicated nature of the future industrialized economy of Canada. It would be tragic, indeed, if the present constitution were used as a roadblock as we strive to solve this key aspect to survival as a nation.

In an evolving situation, the Canadian government should keep its options open before a definitive organizational structure is set in place to achieve national objectives. Recognition must be given to the unpredictibility and severity of OPEC policies, the instability in the Middle East, the political and constitutional debates in Canada, the unresolved issues in the distribution of energy revenues, and the overall economic and political impact of any energy strategy to be pursued. No one plan or program can anticipate the specific dilemmas that any or all of these variable factors may pose at a given moment in time. Any single doctrinaire solution, therefore, carries with it the possibility, if not the likelihood, of being out of focus with at least some existing realities. Pragmatic, rather than dogmatic, responses will be required to meet the challenges. Nevertheless, imaginative and decisive steps will be required if Canada's energy future is to be secured.

In the current situation many options may be considered and certainly, circumstances as they evolve will call for modifications in energy planning proposals. One proposal that is, I submit, worthy of very serious consideration is the creation of a National Energy Corporation (NEC). In many respects, its functions would be somewhat parallel to those of the wartime Ministry of Munitions and Supply. The NEC would be a central clearinghouse for requests for future energy supplies required by the various regions and sectors of the economy. In complying with such requests in an energy-deficient situation, the NEC would judge their reasonableness and allocate resources to those warranting service, using existing supplies to maximum efficiency. In an ever-tightening market, the NEC would allocate or ration scarce commodities and arrange for the supply of substitutes, if they were available. If not, it would direct a course of action judged to be the best compromise among the competing interests. The NEC would consult continuously with industry and government.

The NEC would be charged with the responsibility for nationwide long-range energy supply planning and for recommending to the federal government appropriate national energy policies. The government in turn would discuss such policies with the provinces, modify them as agreed, present them to parliament, and implement them with the force of law where necessary.

The NEC would delegate project operating responsibility to the maximum possible degree. Only essential functions would be centralized. Compliance with national standards and objectives would be achieved through financial and operating audits. Provincial and local input would be encouraged and merged into a national plan designed to provide the highest degree of security of supply and equitable distribution for all regions of the country. The NEC would carry out its principal functions by contracting for and purchasing energy supplies from producers or transmitters and, in turn, selling same to purchasers or distributors. In this respect it would have general powers similar to those of the Alberta Petroleum Marketing Commission. It would control and manage energy commodities on a national basis by setting the price. In the case of crude oil, the price would be established nationally on the basis of the weighted average cost of the various sources of supply plus transportation costs.

The NEC would be the action-oriented federal agency through which an agreed upon federal energy supply plan would be administered. For example, on the supply side, it would prepare estimates of the skilled manpower requirements of construction projects and pass those estimates along to the appropriate federal and provincial authorities who, in turn, would take the necessary steps to encourage the development of a program to train the various craftsmen. On the demand side, in addition to furthering energy conservation, the NEC might encourage provincial electric authorities to undertake to serve certain consumer needs previously met from declining supplies of petroleum products; when necessary, federal legislation or regulations might be required to achieve national objectives.

The NEC would not, however, replace the National Energy Board (NEB) or Petro-Canada. The NEB would retain its responsibilities to regulate oil and gas exports as well as interprovincial and international pipelines and power lines and its jurisdiction over pipeline tariffs and tolls; its functions would be expanded to include the determination of price of all forms of energy, where impossible to fix through negotiation. Petro-Canada would still operate as an exploration and producing company, providing the federal government and the NEC with important industry information. Its role could be expanded as a supplier-contractor of energy to the NEC. If so, it would act on a cost-of-service basis, which would include a return on investment.

Briefly, some of the major undertakings of the NEC would be to:

- study Canadian domestic markets for various forms of energy on a regional and sectoral basis;
- prepare forecasts of future needs having in mind the anticipated availability, cost, and substitutability of various energy forms and the importance of conservation and improved efficiency;
- study the present and assured future sources of supply that can be relied upon to deliver at a particular level of output over an extended period of time;
- forecast requirements for additional supplies and recommend the best or most likely sources for procurement;
- examine all possibilities for substituting renewable energy forms in markets served by non-renewables;
- develop a comprehensive national energy conservation program, co-ordinating the energy requirements of the various regions and sectors to assist in developing optimum national plans and assured regional supplies;
- with assistance from industry, prepare preliminary estimates of the cost of developing and delivering new energy supplies and recommend appropriate pricing;
- negotiate draft contracts with producers;
- after government approval, award or allocate the responsibility for developing a particular new energy supply source to either a private sector or crown-owned entity;
- monitor the performance of all existing and new energy supply systems including sources of imports and exports, if any;
- develop long-range plans for moving from depleting and unsustainable non-renewable energy resources to a society based on sustainable supplies of renewable energy;
- act as a national centre for energy research and development, which probably would be conducted on a regional basis; and

122

- act to ensure Canadian control over all forms of energy supply and delivery.

Many advantages would emerge from the establishment of the NEC. Through co-ordinated planning the possibility of disruptive future energy shortages would be minimized and energy supply projects would be developed on a timetable geared to Canadian needs, rather than the impossible to satisfy demands of the United States. Overall national needs would be integrated with those of specific regions or new markets, and dwindling stocks of non-renewable resources would be managed for the benefit of this and future generations. An orderly transition from non-renewable to renewable sources of energy could also be effected. Allocation of essential resources for specific end uses would be rationalized on the basis of need rather than wealth. Further, while achieving the benefits of bringing all energy resources under one central administration, it would also actively involve the provinces and regions in the planning and operating phases of developments. The NEC would be able to advise governments first hand of significant developments in the energy field and recommend policy shifts as justified by perceptions and events, sooner rather than later. It would also be the vehicle for centralizing dealings with U.S. entities and for negotiating mutually advantageous energy exchanges and could provide the means of gaining control of the now foreign-dominated industry.

Spokesmen for the oil industry and others with interests in the existing system can be expected to oppose vigorously the concept of a National Energy Corporation. In the past, however, government has intervened in the Canadian economy when it was necessary to initiate plans or projects that were either too large to be carried out by the private sector or could not be delegated appropriately to private industry or were so important to the nation that nothing less than top-level government management was essential to achieve the fundamental objective being sought (see Appendix). For example, the government intervened during the war to ensure essential supplies and matériel would be available. The federal government also undertook to operate rail and air services when it was clear that private industry was unable to do so. Ontario Hydro was established to bring electric energy in an orderly fashion at cost to the citizens of that province, and this model has been followed in other provincial jurisdictions. Some countries have nationalized enterprises in the oil industry. Many other examples might be cited but the above should be sufficient to develop the argument that no case can be made to the effect that only the private sector should be involved in new energy projects. In light of the failure or the inability of the petroleum industry to maintain adequate life indices of supply for oil and gas, the opposite case is readily established. Canada should not be deterred by the threats of non-co-operation that might emerge from the unregulated petroleum industry. Nor should it be swayed by the arguments from the industry that regulation of profits will kill imagination and initiative.[8] Regulated industries, such as electric utilities and pipelines, have been highly innovative and successful in reducing unit costs through improved technology and operating efficiencies. Conscientious management in the oil industry can be expected to respond in the same manner.

The National Energy Corporation at Work: The Tar Sands as a Key Resource

Over the next fifty years Canada must move from its current reliance on rapidly depleting non-renewable energy resources to a sustainable energy base. It is urgent that this move is begun earnestly and very soon. At the same time the serious petroleum shortages looming in the 1980s must be frontally addressed. Consequently, Canada must manage its existing non-renewable energy resources in such a way that, to the maximum extent possible, both the needs of the next thirty years are met and that the bridge to an energy future based on non-depleting resources is built. This will depend upon effective management of both energy demand and supply.

Fortunately, Canada's potential for creating energy self-sufficiency and managing its own energy destiny is almost unique in the western world. This country possesses large, though finite, amounts of recoverable energy resources in the form of tar sands, heavy oil, and coal deposits. While the tar sands do not offer a solution of unlimited duration, in combination with a program of energy conservation in the near term and a long-range demand and supply orientation, they can provide an essential transitional energy resource. That they are not being developed on a schedule that will lessen Canada's present dependency on offshore crude oil is obvious (see Chart 3-7). Even if the Alsands and Cold Lake projects were to proceed as quickly as possible, the nation's oil supply deficit would still grow at an alarming pace throughout the 1980s and beyond.

Unfortunately, the private sector petroleum industry with its huge financial and manpower resources is doing very little and certainly achieving very little, in levelling off the dropping oil and gas life indices. At a time when the emphasis should be placed on developing tar sands production, it is particularly disconcerting to see the industry devoting much managerial time and money to pressing governments and regulatory authorities to increase the present high level of natural

124

gas exported to the United States. If the industry is successful in its endeavour to step up exports – and there is every indication it will be – the decline of the gas index can only steepen (Chart 3-11) and further reduce future supplies available for Canadians.

The industry, which has managed to build just one new tar sands plant (Syncrude) in the past ten years, and that with considerable government assistance, occasionally makes reference to a stepped-up program. The 1979 chairman of the Canadian Petroleum Association observed that a $4 billion oil sands plant should be built every two and a half years and that on that basis "we could be energy self-sufficient from 1995 onward." He also has said that "governments should ease up on front-end royalty and taxation loads". But one cannot help but get the impression that the industry is playing games with governments, seeking higher prices along with reduced royalties and taxes in return for proceeding with a limited program that will come nowhere near meeting Canada's needs. While future domestic supply inadequacies will make higher industry profits possible because consumers will pay virtually anything for crucial energy supplies, it is not a situation governments will be able to face with equanimity.

Obviously a much more ambitious development program than industry hypothesizes is necessary. Chart 6-1 (Program A) envisages the initiation every three years of one new 125,000 barrels per day mining-type oil sands plant with a useful life of thirty years, with work on the first one commencing in 1980. Even if such an accelerated program were undertaken immediately, the magnitude of the forecast supply deficit would continue to increase until it reached 450 million barrels per year (about 1,250,000 bpd) in the year 2009. A minor – probably less than 10 per cent – decline in the deficit is forecast if the progam were continued to 2025. Such a program, by itself, would fall a long way short of meeting a goal of self-sufficiency in petroleum energy, even when the nation's dependency on crude oil and equivalents is assumed to fall from 45 per cent of total energy needs in 1975 to 25 per cent in 2025. Program A should be capable of meeting about 50 per cent of these lowered requirements in the years following 2010.

Program B in Chart 6-2 assumes that it would be possible to gear up the essential sectors of the Canadian economy so that work could begin on one new 125,000 barrels per day mining-type oil sands plant every year, commencing in 1980. The maximum number of plants operating at any one time would be seventeen. If such a far-reaching objective could be achieved, petroleum self-sufficiency could be attained by about 1995, again on the basis of a much scaled down demand growth and the substitution of electricity in many markets now served by petroleum. Self-sufficiency could be maintained for seven or eight

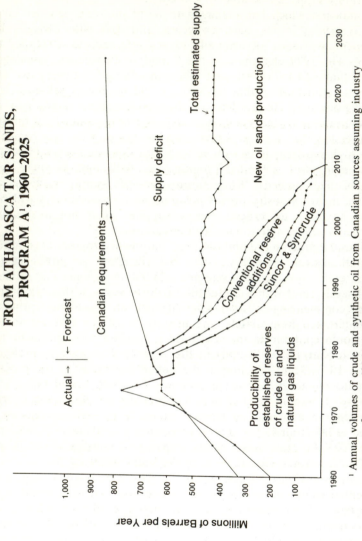

CHART 6-1
PROPOSAL FOR DEVELOPMENT OF SYNTHETIC CRUDE OIL FROM ATHABASCA TAR SANDS, PROGRAM A[1], 1960–2025

Millions of Barrels per Year

Actual → | ← Forecast

Canadian requirements

Supply deficit

Total estimated supply

New oil sands production

Conventional reserve additions

Suncor & Syncrude

Producibility of established reserves of crude oil and natural gas liquids

[1] Annual volumes of crude and synthetic oil from Canadian sources assuming industry program of one new 125,000 bpd oil sands plant every three years.

Source: Based on data from National Energy Board, *Canadian Oil Supply and Requirements, 1978* (Ottawa, 1979).

years following which production would fall rather rapidly, since it would not be economic to build new facilities because of the limited remaining mineable reserves. Under this program, 97 per cent of the mineable tar sands reserves of 22.5 billion barrels theoretically would have been recovered by 2025.[9]

This is, of course, a theoretical calculation to determine whether self-sufficiency for Canada might indeed be possible using the mineable tar sands reserves and today's technology. The answer appears to be a highly qualified "yes". However, the calculations do not take into account the environmental problems such a program would create; nor has a study been done on the huge demands for skilled manpower the program would make on the human resources of the country. A continuous workforce of at least 25,000 would be needed for the on-going construction phases of the program, and requirements for trained operating personnel to run the gigantic plants would be constantly growing. A careful assessment of the educational and training facilities required to turn out craftworkers and tradesmen should be conducted. Similarly, a review of Canadian manufacturing facilities and their capacity for expansion should reveal the potential for domestic firms to supply the billions of dollars worth of the myriad varieties of equipment such a program would entail. The ability of the universities to graduate the thousands of engineers and other professionals needed would also have to be investigated. An accompanying study of the capability of Canadian engineering and construction firms to design and build the complex facilities should be undertaken.

Yet the economic possibilities such a program would create are exciting to contemplate. A thoroughly studied and intelligently managed development of the mining portion of the Athabasca Tar Sands should result in tremendous economies of scale in the provision of engineering, construction, and equipment manufacturing services. Various regions of Canada could benefit from subcontracts assigned to domestic suppliers willing to create new manufacturing facilities in areas of high unemployment. Assured orders for equipment to go into successive new tar sands plants would provide the basis for the establishment of new factories. Standard designs for various plant units could be adopted in order to avoid "reinventing the wheel" for each new facility. An integrated approach to the provision of infrastructure and community services should avoid costly duplication and less than optimum efficiency.

The financing of such a program should not prove a stumbling block, provided that governments and industry co-operate with each other. In 1979 Canadian consumers contributed an additional $9 billion in price increases on domestic oil and gas production for which they

CHART 6-2
PROPOSAL FOR DEVELOPMENT OF SYNTHETIC CRUDE OIL FROM ATHABASCA TAR SANDS, PROGRAM B[1], 1960–2025

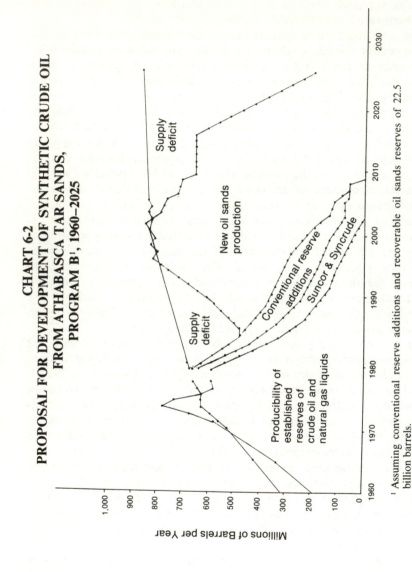

[1] Assuming conventional reserve additions and recoverable oil sands reserves of 22.5 billion barrels.

Source: Based on data from National Energy Board, *Canadian Oil Supply and Requirements, 1978* (Ottawa, 1979).

paid $3 billion in 1973 (see Charts 5-1 and 5-3); in 1980 this figure will probably rise to a minimum of $11 billion. It is difficult to see why at least half of this huge additional revenue stream could not be diverted to fund the capital cost of one new tar sands plant annually, assuming such plants cost in the neighbourhood of $5 billion each.

If the fifteen plant tar sands program were financed in this fashion, each investment could be written off in the year in which it was made. Because the capital would have been provided by the people of Canada, it would be inequitable to charge them an annual return on their own money when calculating the cost of tar sands synthetic oil production. Therefore the total cost of such production would be much lower than that demanded by the oil industry, since there would be no need to provide for return on investment – typically about 20 per cent – or annual depreciation installments. The selling price per barrel of synthetic oil could then be as low as the sum of the annual operating, maintenance, administration, and royalty expenses divided by the number of barrels produced. Such a pricing approach would leave considerable latitude for the addition of excise taxes or other forms of levies to fund in situ research and development programs and the renewable energy projects that are essential if Canada is to move to a secure energy future.

One of the major difficulties with the approach of adopting "world" prices for tar sands production is that very few creative initiatives are now being undertaken as industry and governments jockey for more profitable positions. Industry complains of the "uncertainties" and governments vie for bigger slices of the revenue dollar, while the average Canadian citizen stands helplessly by. Some of the uncertainties could be removed by adopting a cost-based approach for production pricing with project financing as proposed above so that plant operators would be guaranteed the recovery of their costs in the same manner as today's electric utilities are assured of being reimbursed for their expenses. Governments should reconcile their responsibilities on constructive and equitable bases in the interests of all Canadians.

Another difficulty, of course, is the open-ended nature of "world" prices. OPEC increased its cartel price from about $13 in 1978 to $32 per barrel in June 1980, a punitive 150 per cent. Other exporting nations such as Mexico charge even more. Because of their dependency on petroleum fuels, few importing nations can do much short of military action to alter their circumstances. While one can understand the oil companies' interest in having synthetic oil prices tied to such a benchmark, a requirement that Canadian users sign a virtual blank cheque in favour of the industry obviously is quite unfair. For example, the pioneering Great Canadian Oil Sands plant was marginally profitable for the first time in 1974 when its production sold for $6.50 per barrel.[10] And Suncor Inc., which emerged from the 1979 amalgamation of GCOS and Sun Oil Co., reported that $68 million of its 1979 profit increase of $112 million resulted from its synthetic oil production receiving the "world" price beginning in April 1979. Reports from Ottawa indicate the federal government is considering ending the policy of automatically paying "world" oil prices for production from tar sands mining plants, because it is concerned that "world" prices are out of control and therefore inappropriate. As might be expected, immediate protests arose from the oil industry and the Alberta government and opinions vary about what constitutes a fair price for tar sands production.

To make a program such as B possible, governments must intervene directly. All presently undeveloped tar sands and heavy oil leases should be taken into the public domain with return of all lease rentals accrued and appropriate interest. Future development would be undertaken under public control, utilizing private sector entities as contractors in much the same way as the various aspects of the $15 billion James Bay project were handled by the Quebec government and Hydro Quebec. If the multinational oil companies were not prepared to operate on this basis, they would be excused from the program and the country. Canadian-owned entities would be encouraged to expand or crown corporations could be created by the federal or provincial governments to ensure production of an essential resource.

This brief treatment of some of the important aspects of an integrated approach to tar sands development touches only on the larger issues and benefits that would emerge as the program went forward. Obviously in undertaking an endeavour that is so crucial and so massive, there will be problems. But the goal of energy self-sufficiency is so important and so essential for national survival that the battle must be joined. For far too long Canada has drifted on the empty promises of the petroleum industry and the mistaken belief that somehow high prices for present-day low-cost production is a solution to the energy crisis confronting the nation.

For energy, the objective is to ensure adequate supply for national needs at reasonable prices essentially forever. In an energy-intensive world now dependent on dwindling reserves of non-renewable resources, the achievement of such an objective will be difficult and challenging but should not be beyond the reach of a dedicated nation with a sense of purpose.

When this is coupled with the need to reduce the balance of payments deficit, lower unemployment, curb the growth in foreign ownership of Canadian resources, reduce the rate of inflation and, above all,

130

do everything possible to ensure future energy supplies needed to cope with this hostile climate, the case for a National Energy Corporation or somewhat similar mechanism becomes overwhelming. All that is required is a recognition of the seriousness of the challenge facing Canada and the political will to get on with the job.

Summary of Conclusions and Recommendations
Conclusions
- The Canadian economy is dependent on energy for survival. But the present heavy reliance on fossil fuels cannot be sustained for long, because the capacity of non-renewable sources to maintain today's per capita level of energy consumption is very much in doubt. Major painful adjustments are inevitable as society makes the transition from non-renewable to renewable energy sources.
- Despite high energy prices and serious conservation efforts, energy requirements are forecast to continue to grow, albeit at much slower rates than historically.
- Oil and gas, which now supply 65 per cent of the nation's energy needs, will likely continue to be the major energy sources for the next forty-five years, provided supplies are available.
- Canada's crude oil supply outlook is extremely precarious. Relatively assured domestic production will amount to only one-third of estimated requirements by 1990. If forecast reserves additions materialize and two new non-conventional oil developments proceed on schedule, total projected domestic supply will amount to only 62 per cent of requirements in 1990 and 35 per cent of them in 2000. Reserves now in sight will be exhausted in thirty years.
- Oil imports cannot be expected to resolve Canada's problem. World crude oil production already may well have peaked, and imports, which now supply 30 per cent of Canadian requirements, will become more uncertain, extremely costly, and eventually unavailable.
- The domestic natural gas supply/demand outlook is somewhat better than that for crude oil but gives no reason for complacency. If presently forecast reserves additions materialize and gas fields perform as predicted, Southern Basin supplies will meet projected Canadian natural gas demand until the mid-1990s, after which supply deficits will grow rapidly. Conversely, if the substantial reserves additions expected are not forthcoming, shortages will materialize sooner and will be larger. Known Mackenzie Delta gas reserves do not affect the supply outlook materially.
- The reason for this gloomy outlook is that despite the large wellhead price increases for oil and gas in the 1970s, combined re-

serves declined; that is, production including exports, exceeded reserves additions from new discoveries, field extensions, and enhanced recovery techniques. It appears that readily available alternative energy sources will not fulfil future requirements either.

- While uranium supply/demand balances are difficult to analyse because of the limited data base, available information suggests that Canada's known uranium reserves will fall far short of meeting the fuelling demands for a substantial generating program in the 1975–2025 period.

- Canada's recoverable coal reserves are modest, particularly compared with those of the United States. If known recoverable domestic reserves were developed and utilized to contribute a 13 per cent of the share of total forecast energy demand, they would be exhausted by 2025.

- Most of the accessible sites suitable for the generation of hydroelectric energy in Canada have already been developed. Because of this, it is forecast that the share of hydraulic energy will decline from 22 per cent in 1975 to 13 per cent of the country's still growing total energy needs in 2025.

- The present system of private sector domination and provincial control for pacing developments in the oil and gas industry has led to skyrocketing prices and rapidly declining life indices presaging imminent shortages.

- A single policy of pushing oil and gas prices ever higher has not worked in bringing on adequate new reserves. Nor logically can it be expected to work when dealing with depleting non-renewable resources in thoroughly explored geological basins. Furthermore, adoption of the high-price scenario has been inflationary, weakened the manufacturing sector, added to unemployment, pushed up transportation costs, increased the level of foreign ownership of the Canadian economy, contributed to the balance-of-payments deficit, and has been grossly unfair to consumers.

- National energy policies to date have been almost totally ineffective in protecting the long-term interests of Canadians. Energy supply planning has been deficient as forecasts of future supply, which have been based on information and opinions put forward by the petroleum industry, have been consistently wrong.

- Reliance on the private sector, largely the foreign-controlled petroleum industry, has resulted in excessive exports of Canada's conventional oil and gas reserves. This, in turn, has led to the present precarious energy supply outlook for Canadians and the country's vulnerability to reductions in delivery of offshore oil supplies.

132

- Ultimately, when fossil fuels are exhausted, society will have to rely almost exclusively on renewable sources of energy such as solar, wind, biomass, and perhaps fusion power if the process can be controlled and is economic. In the meantime, Canada is blessed with a large resource base of tar sands and heavy oils, the development of which will provide time to plan and manage the painful transition from today's unsustainable dependency on conventional oil and gas, coal, and uranium. However, there is not a moment to lose in tackling this formidable challenge.
- Preparation of a comprehensive national energy supply plan, embracing all energy forms including renewables and covering every region and market, is a basic first step in the development of intelligent and effective Canadian energy policies.
- The full resources of both the public and private sectors will have to be mobilized for energy supply purposes on a carefully planned and integrated basis if Canada is to achieve energy self-sufficiency and reasonable living standards for its people.
- An integrated program for the rapid development of mineable tar sands reserves appears to be the logical first candidate for minimizing the crippling energy shortages now in sight for the 1980s and 1990s. Even with such a program and the co-operation of all concerned, self-sufficiency in crude oil could not be achieved before 1995.
- At the same time, it is essential that research and development of renewable energy sources and the commercialization of in situ tar sands recovery projects be given high priority.
- Constitutional issues will have to be resolved in a manner that provides the federal government with the necessary powers and authority required to provide national solutions and to meet national needs. Comprehensive resource development planning at the federal level is the only hope of achieving energy self-sufficiency. Project execution and operation should be delegated or allocated to regional authorities. Close co-operation between all levels of government and private sector groups will be essential.
- While only the senior government has the capacity and the authority – potentially, at least – to resolve the rapidly deteriorating prospects for adequate energy supplies for Canadians, the opportunities for private sector participation in the required projects and developments are great indeed. With reasonably assured energy supplies at equitable prices in sight, Canada could enter upon a new and prosperously constructive era involving domestically rather than foreign-owned corporations.

Recommendations

- Policies should be developed immediately to ensure adequate supplies of energy for Canadians in the medium term and to allow this country to make the transition from dependence on non-renewable hydrocarbon sources to renewables in the longer term, as effectively as possible.
- All energy resource planning and development should be placed under federal jurisdiction. To this end a National Energy Corporation or similar government authority reporting to the appropriate minister should be constituted. Through this agency, governments and the private sector could co-ordinate both the supply of and demand for energy. Development and operating control would be delegated to provincial authorities; resource owners would receive appropriate royalties; and environmental and socioeconomic concerns would be accorded proper consideration.
- Conservation should be encouraged and demand for scarce energy resources should be controlled by allocating them to priority uses and by equitable rationing.
- All energy commodities should be priced on a cost-related basis. Prices would include all legitimately incurred costs, royalties paid to lessors, and reasonable returns on approved capital investments.
- Additional capital should be made available for energy research and development and for the financing of new energy supply projects through levies of excise taxes on current production on top of the cost-based energy prices.
- New developments should be structured so that expanded energy corporations will be Canadian rather than foreign controlled in order that the benefits will accrue essentially to Canadians.
- A national concensus should be developed on Canada's objectives and priorities. Energy supply planning should be integrated with national economic goals. An effective economic and industrial strategy soundly based on the nation's resources could achieve a much lower rate of inflation, reduced unemployment, major improvements in the balance of international payments, and ultimately a secure future for the coming generations of Canadians.

Appendix

Precedents for Government Initiative

Several examples of precedents for government initiative are cited here.

Canadian Mobilization for the Second World War

C.D. Howe, as minister of munitions and supply, foresaw the need for large quantities of armaments and other vital matériel and mobilized Canadian resources and manufacturing capability in a timely fashion to meet the requirements of not only this nation but Britain as well. He was the moving force in creating new crown companies, such as Polymer at Sarnia for the manufacture of synthetic rubber. To enable him to carry out his duties, he was given broad powers under the Munitions and Supply Act and the War Measures Act. The provinces were forced to concede their jurisdiction over resources to the central government so there was no consitutional barrier to getting the job done.[1] The success of his efforts does not need to be described here. It is sufficient to point out what Canada is capable of doing through centralized planning and action when competent people are in charge and an appropriate legislative framework is in existence.

Ontario Hydro

As Ontario developed and urbanized in the early 1900s the demand for electric energy increased rapidly. Privately owned power interests dominated the scene but were in constant battle with municipal governments over rights-of-way, service, and rates.[2] In 1906 the Conservative government of Ontario set up the Hydro-Electric Power Commission with Adam Beck as chairman. By 1910 it was in operation as the world's first publicly-owned hydro-electric company, and by 1917 it was the world's largest. It developed low-cost electric energy at Niagara Falls and distributed it throughout southern Ontario. It has since built and operated a highly sophisticated system of generating plants utilizing coal, oil, natural gas, and nuclear-fired stations.

Mexico and Venezuela

While this study does not recommend nationalizing the oil industry, it is of interest to observe that these two producing countries have done so with great success. Domestic consumers in Mexico and Venezuela pay much lower prices for petroleum products than would result if crude oil for local use were sold at the cartel or "world" price. In the case of Mexico, recent important discoveries have resulted in that country's crude oil reserves being increased to 45 billion barrels, about seven times Canada's conventional reserves.[3] But, as previously mentioned, Mexico plans to restrain producing rates to 2.25 million barrels per day in order to stretch the useful life of its presently known reserves to fifty years or more. National oil companies, managing resources in the national interest are now very much the rule except in the United States and Canada.

Hydro-Québec

This government-owned energy company recently commissioned the LG 2 generating station as part of the first phase of the $15 billion James Bay project. It is most unlikely that such a development ever could have been financed by the private sector, for it is just too large and private companies would have been unable to come up with completion guarantees or methods of meeting cost overruns satisfactory to the lending institutions. Government backing is the only way whereby such large and complex projects can be financed.

Tennessee Valley Authority

The largest electric utility in the private enterprise oriented United States is a government owned one, the Tennessee Valley Authority. Originally developed to use the stream flow in the Tennessee River to generate hydro-electric energy in a series of generating stations built in conjunction with flood control and marine navigation dams, TVA has expanded tremendously with coal-fired and nuclear-powered plants supplying electricity to a large area in the southeastern states. General support for the private enterprise systems did not prevent U.S. legislators from authorizing the government-owned TVA system from the outset.

U.S. Energy Supply Planning

It should be noted that President Carter's latest energy plan proposes two new federal government agencies to help improve the supply outlook. The first is an Energy Security Corporation to develop America's own alternative sources of fuel to replace 2.5 million barrels of im-

136

ported oil per day by 1990. The second is an Energy Mobilization Board, which would have the responsibility and the authority to cut through red tape and roadblocks to get the various jobs done. Canada should do no less and, indeed, because of the present lack of domestic ownership and control of the key petroleum industry, must do more.

Notes

Chapter 1

[1] Statistics Canada, *Human Activity and Environment,* Cat. 11-509E, p. 127.

[2] *Ibid.,* Table 7.10.

[3] Not to be confused with primary energy, which is the available energy content of the natural resource. Secondary energy is the amount of energy delivered to the final consumer. The difference between the two is the energy lost in conversion and in the process of supply. See J.E. Gander and F.W. Belaire, *Energy Futures for Canadians* (LEAP) (Ottawa: Energy, Mines and Resources Canada, 1978), p. 303.

[4] Correspondence between the author and Hon. J. J. Greene, Minister of Energy, Mines and Resources, July 1971.

[5] Imperial Oil Limited, *Annual Report,* 1972, p. 8.

[6] Imperial Oil Limited, Annual Report, 1973, pp. 3,4.

[7] Energy, Mines and Resources Canada, *An Energy Policy for Canada* (Ottawa, 1973), p. 92.

[8] Canadian Petroleum Association, *Report of the Reserves Committee, 1977,* Table 4.

[9] Energy, Mines and Resources Canada, *An Energy Strategy for Canada* (Ottawa, 1976), pp. 73-91.

[10] Canadian Petroleum Association, *Report of the Reserves Committee, 1977-1978,* and *1979,* Table 4.

[11] Canadian Petroleum Association, *Report of the Reserves Committee, 1978,* Table 13.

[12] National Energy Board, *Annual Report, 1979* (Ottawa, 1980), pp. 15-17.

Chapter 2

[1] See National Energy Board, *Gas Report* (Ottawa, 1979), Table 3-2, p. 45.

[2] Energy, Mines and Resources Canada, *An Energy Strategy for Canada* (Ottawa, 1976), p. 90.

[3] National Energy Board, *Oil Report* (Ottawa, 1978), p. 94.

[4] National Energy Board, *Gas Report* (Ottawa, 1979), p. 45.

[5] Energy, Mines and Resources Canada, *Energy Conservation in Canada: Programs and Perspectives* (Ottawa, 1977), p. 10.

[6] *Ibid.,* p. 56.

[7] *Energy Conservation in Canada,* while not projecting a rate of 2 per cent growth, stated that it was possible to attain this rate to 1990 under reasonable assumptions and that a much lower rate was possible after that.

[8] Lovins estimated secondary demand only. His figures were converted to primary energy terms using the LEAP ratio between primary and secondary energy of 1.6 to 1. This may overstate Lovins primary energy demand forecast, given that his supply scenario has a much lower proportion of electricity. See Amory Lovins, "Exploring Energy-Efficient Futures for Canada," in Science Council of Canada, *Conserver Society Notes* 1, 4 (May-June, 1976).

[9] D. Brooks, R. Erdman, and G. Winstanley, *Some Scenarios of Energy Demand in Canada in the Year 2025,* Report of the Demand and Conservation Task Force (Ottawa, 1977), p. 44.

[10] *Ibid.*

[11] R. Stobaugh and D. Yergin (eds.), *Energy Future,* Report of the Energy Project at the Harvard Business School (New York, 1979).

[12] U.S. National Academy of Science, *Energy in Transition* (Washington, 1980). See also Anthony Parisi's review, *New York Times,* January 20, 1980.

[13] The study also looked at a scenario that assumed a "very aggressive" energy conservation program that "deliberately arrived at reduced demand requiring some lifestyle changes." The energy demand in this scenario was reduced 25 per cent from 1975 to 53.2 quads. Parisi, *New York Times.*

[14] See, for example, Carter Henderson, *The Inevitability of Petroleum Rationing in the United States* (Princeton, 1978).

[15] Not all the processes used in arriving at the demand forecasts are detailed in the report, though the letter of transmittal states that the authors engaged in extensive discussions with their departmental colleagues and with representatives of other federal departments and agencies, provincial officials, and industry spokesmen.

[16] National Energy Board, *Oil Report,* p. 95; *Gas Report,* p. 45.

[17] LEAP report, p. 138.

[18] *Ibid.,* p. 160.

Chapter 3

[1] National Energy Board, *Canadian Natural Gas Supply and Requirements* (Ottawa, 1979), Table 3-4, p. 46.

[2] *Ibid.*

[3] Carroll L. Wilson, *Energy: Global Prospects, 1985-2000,* Report of the Workshop on Alternative Energy Strategies (New York, 1977), p. 140.

[4] See *Globe and Mail,* April 17, 1979.

[5] John R. Kiely "World Energy in the Long-Range Future," presentation to the Fifth Canadian National Energy Forum, Calgary, November 19, 1979.

[6] *Globe and Mail,* March 22, 1979.

[7] "Annual Review and Forecast," *Oilweek,* February 12, 1979.

[8] "Mid year Review and Forecast," *Oilweek,* July 28, 1980.

[9] Richard Nehring, *Giant Oil Fields and World Oil Reserves* (New York, 1978).

[10] DeGolyer and MacNaughton, *Twentieth Century Petroleum Statistics* (Dallas, 1977), Table 1.

[11] National Energy Board, *Oil Report* (Ottawa, 1978), p. 234.

[12] Nehring, *Giant Oil Fields.*

[13] Based on data from the Canadian Petroleum Association. Data for 1978 and 1979 are not shown as the CPA announced in 1979 that it was discontinuing publishing its traditional "proved" reserves numbers in favour of showing "probable" reserves, which includes the "proved" category, and is now adopting the term "established."

[14] NEB, *Oil Report,* p.4.

[15] National Energy Board, *Canadian Oil Supply and Requirements* (Ottawa, 1978).

[16] *Globe and Mail,* May 16, 1979.

[17] *Toronto Star,* March 9, 1979 and August 19, 1980.

[18] NEB, *Oil Report,* p. 68.

[19] DeGolyer and MacNaughton, *Twentieth Century Petroleum Statistics* (Dallas, 1977) Table 80.

[20] Phillips Petroleum Co. and State of Wisconsin, 347 U.S. 672, 74 S. Ct. 794 (1954).

[21] American Gas Association, *Gas Facts* 1978, Table 97.

[22] *Ibid,* Table 64.

[23] *Ibid,* Table 70.

[24] *Ibid,* Table 97.

[25] See Nehring, *Giant Oil Fields.*

[26] Imperial Oil Limited, *Annual Report,* 1978, p. 29.

[27] Hudson's Bay Oil and Gas Company Limited, *Annual Report,* 1978, p. 31.

[28] Alberta Energy Resources Conservation Board, *The Supply of and Demand for Alberta Gas* (Calgary, 1978).

[29] National Energy Board, *Canadian Natural Gas Supply and Requirements* (Ottawa, 1979).

[30] National Energy Board Act, 1959, c. 46, S. 1, section 83.

[31] NEB, *Canadian Natural Gas Supply and Requirements,* pp. 5, 100, 101.

[32] *Ibid.,* p. 142.

[33] Alberta Energy Resources Conservation Board, *Conservation in Alberta 1978* (Calgary, 1979) and *Conservation in Alberta 1979,* (Calgary, 1980).

[34] S. L. Ross, "Countermeasures for Oil Spills in Canadian Arctic Waters: The Arctic Marine Oil Spill Program", paper presented to Arctic Marine Technical Seminar, (Edmonton, June 1980).

[35] *Conservation in Alberta,* 1978 and 1979, pp. 13 and 10 respectively.

[36] My efforts to obtain a provincial breakdown of CPA's statistics have been unsuccessful, but press reports indicate the location of the growth. *Oilweek,* March 31, 1980, p. 11.

[37] NEB, *Canadian Natural Gas Supply and Requirements,* p. 33.

[38] Terence Armstrong, "Soviet Capabilities in Arctic Marine Transport", paper delivered to conference of Canadian Arctic Resources Committee, University of Cambridge, March 1979.

[39] NEB, *Canadian Natural Gas Supply and Requirements,* p. 36.

[40] *Ibid.*

[41] *Globe and Mail,* June 17, 1980.

[42] *Globe and Mail,* July 5, 1980.

Chapter 4

1 The reader seeking more information on these key aspects of nuclear power is referred to Royal Commission on Electric Power Planning in Ontario, (RCEPP) *A Race Against Time,* Interim Report on Nuclear Power in Ontario, (Toronto, 1978).

2 World Energy Conference (WEC) *World Energy: Looking Ahead to 2020* (London, 1978).

3 Paper presented by Gordon McNabb, president, Uranium Canada Limited, at *Financial Post* conference, Vancouver, April 1979.

4 *Globe and Mail,* April 11, 1979.

5 *Globe and Mail,* July 11, 1979.

6 RCEPP: *A Race Against Time,* Table 9.4, p. 142.

7 *Ibid.,* p. 139.

8 *Ibid.,* p. 143.

9 Energy, Mines and Resources Canada (EMR), *1977 Assessment of Canada's Uranium Supply and Demand* (Ottawa, 1978), p. 7, adjusted for reliability by factors of 1.0, 0.8, and 0.7 respectively.

10 *Ibid.,* pp. 22, 23.

11 RCEPP, *A Race Against Time,* p. 143.

12 Carroll L. Wilson, *Energy: Global Prospects, 1986-2000,* Report of the Workshop on Alternative Energy Strategies (New York, 1977).

13 *Ibid.,* pp. 171-2.

14 Energy, Mines and Resources Canada (EMR), *Coal Resources and Reserves of Canada,* ER 79-9 (Ottawa, 1979).

15 *Ibid.,* p. 22.

16 Mineable coal is defined as that portion of measured coal resources in all parts of the country, including those areas in which mining is not currently allowed, that is recoverable using "broad" economic judgments. *Ibid.,* p. 37.

17 J. E. Gander and F. W. Belaire, *Energy Futures for Canadians* (LEAP) (Ottawa: Energy, Mines and Resources Canada, 1978), p. 161.

18 Geothermal energy is not renewable in the sense defined above. However, it does not appear that use of this resource to the extent that seems feasible will reduce the ongoing availability of this energy.

19 Other possibilities include advanced nuclear fission power and nuclear fusion, which has yet to be technically and economically proven.

20 WEC, *World Energy.*

21 LEAP Report, p. 133.

22 Statistics Canada, *Household Facilities and Appliances,* Cat. 64-202.

23 Barry Commoner, "The Solar Transition," *New Yorker,* April 23, 30, 1979.

24 LEAP Report, p. 160.

25 Science Council of Canada, *Roads to Energy Self-Reliance: The Necessary National Demonstrations* (Ottawa, 1979).

26 Amory Lovins, "Exploring Energy-Efficient Futures for Canada," in Science Council of Canada, *Conserver Society Notes* 1, 4 (May-June 1976).

27 John Robinson *Et al., Canadian Energy Futures: An Investigation of Alternative Energy Futures,* Workgroup on Canadian Energy Policy, Faculty of Environmental Studies, York University, 1977.

Chapter 5

[1] J. E. Gander and F. W. Belaire, *Energy Futures for Canadians* (LEAP) (Ottawa: Energy, Mines and Resources Canada, 1978), p. 160.

[2] *Ibid.*

[3] Ontario Royal Commission on Electric Power Planning, *A Race Against Time,* Interim Report on Nuclear Power (Toronto 1978), Compendium of Major Findings, p. xv.

[4] See the prospectus issued on January 17, 1979, by Amoco Canada Petroleum Company Ltd., listing distributions of $364 million during the 1973–78 period to Amoco Canada's shareholder, Standard Oil Company (Indiana).

[5] See Charts 3-6 and 3-11 for wellhead price increases from 1973 to 1978. They continued throughout 1979 and 1980, and latest being a $2.00 per barrel hike imposed unilaterally by Alberta effective August 1, 1980 with a parallel increase in the wellhead price of natural gas of 30 cents per Mcf.

[6] See "The Taxpayer Fattens Dome," *Calgary Herald,* August 22, 1979.

[7] *Ibid.*

[8] *Oilweek,* Annual Review and Forecast, February 11, 1980, p. 39.

[9] National Energy Board Act, Sec. 83(a).

[10] National Energy Board, *Oil Report* (Ottawa 1978), p. 202.

[11] National Energy Board, *Canadian Natural Gas Supply and Requirements* (Ottawa 1979), p. 5.

[12] American Gas Association, *Gas Facts 1978* (Arlington, Va., 1979) Table 97, p. 122; AERCB, *Conservation in Alberta 1978,* Chart 16, p. 12.

[13] Imperial Oil Limited letter dated July 27, 1973 to TransCanada Pipelines setting forth proposal to link the price of natural gas at the Toronto city gate to fuel oil prices.

[14] See Suncor Inc., 1979 *Annual Report,* pp. 7, 32.

[15] *The Globe and Mail,* Toronto, August 1, 1979.

[16] National Energy Board Act, sections 44, 83.

[17] Energy, Mines and Resources Canada, *An Energy Strategy for Canada* (Ottawa, 1976), p. 126.

[18] *Ibid.,* pp. 73, 80.

[19] A submission filed by the Canadian Petroleum Association with the NEB in 1974 calculated the average cost of finding and developing western Canada's oil and gas reserves during the 1947–73 period inclusive as 48 cents per barrel and 8.2 cents per Mcf, respectively. These reserves constitute the bulk of todays' supplies. See Canadian Petroleum Association, *Canadian Natural Gas Supply and Requirements, 1973–95,* prepared by Sherman H. Clark Associates, Table 69, p. 194.

[20] Hudson's Bay Oil and Gas Company Limited, *Annual Report 1978,* pp. 30, 31.

[21] Reported after-tax profits of certain oil companies for 1979, compared with 1978, are as follows: Dome Petroleum, up 45 per cent to $182 million; Gulf Canada, up 47 per cent to $274 million; Imperial Oil, up 50 per cent to $471 million; Shell Canada, up 62 per cent to $243 million; Texaco Canada, up 71 per cent to $264 million; and Suncor Inc., up 194 per cent to $170 million. Other oil companies, wholly owned subsidiaries of foreign parents,

do not report publicly. First quarter profits for 1980 of six major oil companies were reported to be 70 per cent higher than during the comparable period in 1979. See *Toronto Star*, April 28, 1980.

[22] The National Energy Board *Annual Report, 1979* states that consumption of major energy fuels in Canada increased by 7.3 per cent that year and by an average of 4.2 per cent annually in the 1975–79 period, p. 12.

[23] In 1979, Canada's oil imports exceeded exports by about 115 million barrels. At an average differential of $14 per barrel, the net cost of the oil import compensation program was about $1.6 billion. This will increase rapidly in future years, unless positive steps are taken to make Canada self-sufficient in petroleum.

[24] *An Energy Policy for Canada*, (Ottawa 1973), Phase 1, Vol. II, Chap. 3, pp. 72–98. *An Energy Strategy for Canada*, (Ottawa 1976), Chapter 4, pp. 73–91.

[25] *Globe and Mail*, June 26, 1980. "AERCB told higher wellhead price is key to oil recovery."

[26] De Golyer and MacNaughton, *Twentieth Century Petroleum Statistics, 1977* (Dallas, 1978), Table 15.

[27] Revenue figures from Annual Review and Forecast issues of *Oilweek*; Production figures from reports of CPA Reserves Committee.

[28] See *Oilweek* October 22, 1979 report of speech by Premier Peckford of Newfoundland.

Chapter 6

[1] Ontario Royal Commission on Electric Power Planning, *A Race against Time*, Interim Report on Nuclear Power in Ontario (Toronto, 1978).

[2] *Business Latin America*, January 31, 1979, p. 39.

[3] *Globe and Mail*, October 3, 1979, p. 46.

[4] Premier Peter Lougheed, Quebec, August 1979, as reported in the *Toronto Star*.

[5] Energy, Mines and Resources, *An Energy Policy for Canada* (Ottawa, 1973), *An Energy Strategy for Canada* (Ottawa, 1976), and *Energy Futures for Canadians* (Ottawa, 1978). See also National Energy Board, *Canadian Natural Gas Supply and Requirements* (Ottawa, 1979).

[6] Opinion contained in a letter to the author.

[7] *Toronto Star*, October 26, 1979.

[8] *Globe and Mail*, November 2, 1979.

[9] Alberta Energy Resources Conservation Board, *Conservation in Alberta 1978* (Calgary 1978), p. 12.

[10] Great Canadian Oil Sands Limited, *Annual Report 1978*, p. 16.

Appendix

[1] Robert Bothwell and William Kilbourn, *C. D. Howe: A Biography* (Toronto, 1979).

[2] *Canada's Illustrated Heritage, 1900–1910* (Toronto, 1978), pp. 177–8.

[3] *Time*, October 8, 1979.